scary news

12 Ways to Raise Joyful Children
When the Headlines are Full of Fear

scary news

*12 Ways to Raise Joyful Children
When the Headlines are Full of Fear*

Lorna Knox

Crystal Clarity Publishers
Nevada City, California

Contributing Editor: Susan Dermond
Interior Design by Sans Serif Inc.
Cover Design by Lisa Lanthall

Printed in Canada

Crystal Clarity Publishers
14618 Tyler Foote Road
Nevada City, CA 95959

800.424.1055 or 530.478.7600
fax: 530.478.7610
Clarity@crystalclarity.com
www.crystalclarity.com

Library of Congress Cataloging-in-Publication Data

Knox, Lorna Ann.
   Scary news: 12 things you can do to raise joyful children when the
headlines are full of fear / Lorna Knox.-- 1st ed.
      p. cm.
   Includes bibliographical references.
   ISBN 1-56589-201-1 (trade paper)
   1. Child rearing. 2. Child psychology. 3. Parenting. 4. Spiritual life.
I. Title: 12 things you can do to raise joyful children when the headlines
are full of fear. II. Title: Twelve things you can do to raise joyful children
when the headlines are full of fear. III. Title.
   HQ769.K55525 2004
   649'.1—dc22
                                                    2004018083

Contents

Introduction

"Being a parent is wonderful, I wouldn't change it for the world." Parenting is indeed full of wonder and rewards that can't be found anywhere else, and in a public opinion poll, 96 percent of the respondents agreed with that statement.[1] Most parents, even in these uncertain times, wouldn't give up their responsibilities for less complicated lives. But more than two-thirds of parents who responded to the same poll felt that their parenting job is a lot harder now than it was for their parents.

Almost all parents responded that they worry about negative influences on their children from many outside sources. That concern is so constant and powerful that it overrides other issues, including worries about money or lack of family time. This concern is probably not surprising if you are parent or spend time with parents. It certainly matches my experience, and that of families I spend time with. We are all trying to protect our children and prepare them for the world in a variety of ways. But there is a constant underlying fear that such efforts are inadequate.

Today's headlines are frightening. Terrorism, war, unemployment, earthquakes, poverty, crime, disease—it seems as if every day brings a new crisis, a new cause for concern, and another reason to fear for the future. The challenge of living with joy and courage when darkness and fear are pressing in from all sides is daunting for almost any adult, especially those who have children.

The daily routines of family life, school, extracurricular activities, and friendships are enough to keep every family occupied and challenged: social skills to learn, academic goals to reach, important values and moral lessons to transmit, and so little time before each child has to become independent and go "out there" where those scary headlines are very real. The pressure on parents can be intense. There is a sense of urgency to get it all done and do it *right*, to make sure our children survive these difficult times and to prepare them to survive as adults in difficult times to come, when we are not with them.

If you are anything like me and like the parents I know, you hope your children will not merely *survive* difficult times, but experience a life of joy, optimism, inner contentment, and love for others, and that they are able to help the next generation experience the same. You probably also worry about your ability to give them what they need to make such an experience happen.

The scary news comes from all directions simultaneously. Whether your children are infants, school age, or grown, issues and current events make you concerned for their safety and their future. In any given week, headlines that affect families with children are too many to count. There is no way to deal with each of them directly, but all present one problem we must deal with—fear.

The scary news headlines feed our fears—fear for our children's safety; for their mental, emotional, and physical health; and for their future. We fear for the state of our schools, for our country, and for the world; and we fear for our own ability to parent in such uncertainty.

Fear can shape our decisions and become the driving force in our lives. The choices we make as parents and the directions our fears take us affect our whole family, whether or not we are aware of it. We can't ignore the headlines and the issues that confront the world; we can't pretend they don't affect our children. But many parents share the same questions: How do I overcome my own anxiety and give my children what they need? Is it possible to live joyfully with everything that is going on in the world today? How can I help my children to be joyful and positive, to live with more love than with more fear?

Yes, it is possible for our children to be joyful and positive in a world full of scary news. However, it is not going to happen without conscious and persistent effort. Presented in this book are twelve specific ways to teach children how to live with joyful appreciation and gain inner strength while growing up in a world full of frightening events and media messages that promote anxiety and fear.

What I propose is really easier than you may think. Teaching children to make decisions based on love instead of on fear is the natural inclination of the heart. Helping them to choose true friends, to act with love for others, and to gain strength and wisdom from experience are goals all parents have expressed in one form or another.

If you are looking for guidance and concrete ways to decrease fear while you increase your family's experience of love, beauty, peace, and joyful appreciation of each day, you will find help within these pages. Every chapter has practical suggestions and advice for leading your family away from fear and toward light and love in all areas of their lives.

Teaching children that scary news is a part of our everyday existence and can be dealt with while still holding onto joy can be done systematically and lovingly. Raising children in this way requires the same clarity and awareness we use to teach them other important skills. Think of parents teaching about the dangers of fast-moving cars. In my city neighborhood I've watched moms and dads deal with the traffic issue in a predictable pattern. First they try to make their children understand that cars share their space and present a danger. Then they place themselves between their children and the street during outside playtime until they feel fairly confident the children will not run into traffic. Years of training and practice crossings occur before parents allow children solo trips across the street, and even then diligent parents are ever watchful. An entirely new phase of learning takes place when as teenagers, children learn to drive and take on the responsibility of watching out for youngsters on the street.

Part One chapters focus on how to create an environment that protects and nurtures children during the vulnerable years of early childhood. Topics cover how to...

1. Understand how much negative and harmful emotional influences permeate daily life
2. Shield children from the harsher realities of life during their vulnerable developing years
3. Create a home that is a haven of peace and safety where joy and optimism can thrive
4. Choose true friends who share strength, courage, and optimism
5. Comfort ourselves and others when needed

Part Two chapters cover the skills needed to deal with negative influences while maintaining confidence and a positive attitude. Topics cover how to...

6. Decide when to take action and defend against a threat
7. Balance intellectual assessment with inner guidance
8. Live in the present without debilitating worry for the future or regret for the past
9. See and appreciate the goodness and beauty that exists around us
10. Act with love for others when faced with fear or helplessness
11. Nurture a spiritual identity
12. Gain strength and wisdom from every experience

These topics are not necessarily steps to take in the order presented. However, there is a logical progression from one step to the next. As you consciously take action in these areas, you will create a life for your family that is joyful and positive. You also take control of negative forces instead of letting them control you. Your children will learn a great deal just from your example and from the environment you create with your efforts, but there are also specific skills you can teach children to prepare them for adult life in an uncertain world.

You may feel confident that you are already using many of these ideas or you may feel you need to work harder on others. You may not need to dramatically change what you are doing now; just raise awareness of your goals and what you are up against. These ideas may be familiar, but have existed only as vague hopes and disjointed pieces that come together by chance instead of by design. All of the topics are on a continuum that reaches far into adulthood; growth and learning doesn't stop at a particular age. As children reach new developmental milestones, their ability to understand and take action in each of these areas will change, as will your opportunities to teach them. These chapters will help you clarify how to make joy and beauty a more tangible part of your life with your children, and how to guide them into adulthood with more confidence and hope.

How do you start? Your loving attention is the most important piece of the entire picture. No matter the age of your children or the circumstances, a reliable, loving, secure relationship with parents and other adults has proven to be the most influential factor in helping children feel safe and confident when faced with situations that provoke anxiety or fear. My hope is that everything in this book will reinforce that fact and reassure you it is true.

The suggestions in the following chapters will do more for children than just minimize the damage done by frightening world events. We can give our children the skills to cope with the scary news *and* have a life filled with light, hope, joy, and appreciation.

1 State Farm Insurance and Family Friendly Programming Forum, 2002. Public Agenda Online, www.publicagenda.org

PART I

*Provide Your Children
with a Positive,
Nurturing Environment*

Chapter 1

A Child's View

Understand how much negative and harmful emotional influences permeate our daily life.

Some may think that disturbing events are taking place with greater frequency now than at other times in our history, but I'm not convinced. Pick a time and a place and look in the history books. Plagues and war, political upheaval, economic collapse, natural disasters, murders, kidnappings, bigotry and racism, drought and floods, crop failures and famine, accidents and disease, poverty and rebellion appear throughout the history of every continent and nation. I think what *is* true is that bad news travels faster than ever before, and there are so many ways scary news can attack our daily lives that it can be a tremendous challenge to keep joy alive under the onslaught.

Ask yourself this question: What is the speed of dark?

The Speed of Dark

The speed of dark is how long it takes to turn on the news, find the talk radio station, drive past a billboard, pick up the newspaper, read the headlines while in the checkout line, flip open a magazine at the doctor's office, greet the neighbor in the driveway, chat with a coworker at the coffee machine. Bad news travels at the speed of dark, and it is very fast. Bad news for an adult is disturbing or saddening, upsetting or alarming. For children, bad news is often simply *scary*.

In the primitive days of human history, communication was primarily by word of mouth. Urgent news was communicated only as fast and as far as feet could run. Then came signal fires, drums, and horses or other animal transportation as people around the world came up with creative ways to carry news more quickly and over longer distances than a runner could manage. The printing press gave us a big leap forward and was followed by the invention of the telegraph and the telephone. By the early nineteenth century a postal system was in place and the world continued to shrink.

It was in the 1930s, when radio had found its way into almost every U.S. living room that the speed of dark increased beyond anything dreamed of. Radio was the first true mass broadcast media and brought information and entertainment to millions. In 1938 it also was the instrument that brought mass hysteria and unprecedented fear to countless listeners. Orson Welles's dramatic fictional broadcast, "War of the Worlds," testifies to the power of scary news and the speed of dark.

Less than twenty years later, television had replaced radio as the most common source of information and the most popular form of home entertainment. Now scary news was seen live, with all the fear and fascination of experiencing it firsthand.

In only one generation after radio, modern–day communication includes satellites, mobile phones, pagers, fax machines, video, palm–size computers, digital technology, and the Internet. Television is no longer just in living rooms; it's turned on in doctors' offices, restaurants, department stores, hair salons, airports, schools, and even automobiles (and not just limousines!). The Internet can be accessed at home, work, cafes, libraries, classrooms, and even through cellular

Unless you live in extreme isolation, information bombards you constantly.

phones. Electronic mail provides instantaneous access to friends and strangers around the world. You can't avoid the electronic billboards lining streets, radios playing in stores and offices, headlines glaring at you in every checkout aisle, and piles of unsolicited mail filling your mailbox.

Unless you live in extreme isolation, information bombards you constantly. The ability to communicate has changed so dramatically that we no longer have to go out of our way to obtain information; we have to protect our children and ourselves from its constant onslaught.

Many joys and advantages are gleaned from our modern communication that I wouldn't want to change. We can access information so easily; if you want to know about the weather in China, the rules for a game of cricket, or the words to an song, you can find the answer almost immediately. When my father told me to "Look it up!" I headed for the set of *Encyclopedia Britannica* or the huge *Webster's* dictionary kept out for those occasions. It is different now. Have you seen your children freeze in the middle of the room, uncertain which way to turn because they have a dozen possible "look it up" options at their fingertips? I have.

Every day we are exposed to countless messages that evoke emotional responses.

Who would want to give back the warm thrill of hearing a loved one's voice from across the world? I know what it looks like to gaze down on our planet from an orbiting space station, thanks to communication technology. My children's best friends moved across the country and they write to one another regularly. But instead of becoming distant pen pals, their friendship has flourished with the help of cell phones, digital video, and e-mail. I homeschool my children with deep gratitude every day for the abundance of resources available to us.

There is another side, however. If we are able to send pictures from a space station, we are able to send pictures from a battlefield; if we use cameras to record birthday parties, we can also use them to record the devastation caused by a tornado or a bomb. News events draw us in and tug at our emotions until they *feel* personal. Millions felt included in the excitement of Princess Diana's spectacular royal wedding, and millions felt grief and loss as the news of her death flashed around the world.

Emotions and Information

The emotions we experience are the key here: Every day we are exposed to countless messages every day that evoke emotional responses. During a few hours we may be hit with media messages designed to elicit fear, revulsion, frustration, anger, helplessness, sympathy, concern, sadness, pride, relief. There is humor, too; however, the laughs are often cold and the humor mean spirited.

We are assimilating more than the information that adds to our knowledge and stimulates our intellect. We are also faced with sorting through the startling flood of emotional messages. Our brains react and process constantly, with only a tiny fraction of the deluge having significance to our survival. The bizarre truth is that usually headlines and billboards and talk show topics have no relevance to who we are or how we conduct our lives.

Think of *your* life—your work, marriage, children, friendships, business, physical health, finances, home environment, education, and creative and spiritual activities and interests that are challenging and rewarding. These activities require your attention and fill your heart with more than enough to keep you occupied. Emotion permeates every moment. But the outside world gives you so much more.

In the sensational language of the modern media, every need is a crisis and every concern a threat. Megan Gunnar, Ph.D., professor of child development at the University of Minnesota, explains that stress exists when we *perceive* a threat and attempt to *defend* against it. To defend against every contrived crisis as if it were a real threat would result in stress at a debilitating level, so we must sort through all the crises and pick our battles. Fortunately, most adults have the experience and cognitive maturity to figure out what is media hype and what is of serious concern that requires thought and action.

Typical parents coming home from work may see several billboards depicting the dangers of drugs, the violence of domestic abuse, and perhaps a political ad urging a vote to "Save Our Schools!" The radio news tells of all the latest scandals and terrorist alerts. The headlines tell of war news and another natural disaster. They see it all while processing the day's events at work and are still able to interpret the information, decide if any of it is a real threat that needs an immediate response, and walk in the door ready to prepare dinner.

Children are bombarded with the same frightening news, emotional messages, and violent realities. But they don't have the experience, the maturity, the knowledge, or the perspective to understand them and deal with them. Their brains are still developing; they don't have a worldview that puts information into a useful context. They are in the process of *creating* their worldview based on their experience.

As our culture has become media rich and media saturated, the lines between fact and fantasy, advertising and propaganda, information and entertainment have become so blurred that they are indistinguishable. Coping with the onslaught of information, emotional manipulation, and grim realities of human behavior in a healthy manner takes a complex array of skills that challenges an intelligent, confident adult. How is a child supposed to discriminate between scary events that are a personal threat and scary events that aren't?

Our children will look to us to give them the skills they need to balance the scary realities with the joys that are just as real.

Living with joy and optimism is a daily struggle in a world where conscious and persistent effort is needed to keep a balanced view of life. The rates of depression and suicide at younger and younger ages would seem to point out that cultivating and keeping a balanced view is a difficult task. The National Institute for Mental Health reports that the age of depression onset is occurring earlier in individuals born in recent decades[1] and that in 2001 suicide was the third leading cause of death in youths age 15–24.[2]

We must understand and accept the fact that technology will continue to advance, bringing advantages and experiences we cannot foresee. But technology does not automatically provide greater understanding; it will always have a negative side. The harsher realities of life will continue to invade our personal space, and media influence will become even more pervasive.

To keep a balanced view of life we must be aware of the positive as well as the negative side and understand that the conditions we are trying to balance will constantly be in motion, requiring continual adjustments. Our children will look to us to give them the skills they need to balance the scary realities with the joys that are just as real.

Suggestions

You may have found yourself crawling around on the floor and looking at the environment from your toddler's height, as suggested by safety experts, to clearly see hazards and make your home child friendly. Now try taking a mental look at your children's environment and note how many negative, emotional, and potentially scary messages they may encounter regularly. Write your observations down.

If you want to take a detailed inventory of media influences, *Dr Dave's Cyberhood; Making Media Choices that Create a Healthy Electronic Environment for Your Kids*, by

David Walsh, Ph.D.[3], has many useful suggestions and even provides forms to fill in. Here are some general ideas:

How many television or computer screens does your child encounter in a typical day?

This question is different from asking how many hours of TV your child watches. Take note of where the screens are, such as waiting rooms, the mall, the barbershop, friends' homes, restaurants, and the library.

How many magazine covers and newspaper pictures does your child see?

Think about the checkout lane at the grocery store, waiting rooms, restaurants, your coffee table, and the pile of mail. If your child can read the headlines, count that as a double experience.

Pay close attention to what your children listen to every day.

Take note of when you play the radio in the car or at home. If the TV is on and your children are not watching, can they hear it? How often are your children within hearing of adult or older sibling conversations? What can they hear as they go to sleep? What can they hear at the grocery store, the orthodontist, while riding the bus?

How many billboards, signs, bumper stickers, and advertisements do you notice with content that could be scary or confusing to a child?

Think about the emotional impact of the pictures and the words you pass by on the way to school and in your neighborhood.

Look around your children's schools and make special note of the messages they are exposed to.

If they attend schools with multiple grade levels, there may be information intended for older children that never is explained or introduced to younger students directly but has an impact nonetheless. Even in preschool and kindergarten classrooms, for some children information intended to educate and prepare may cause anxiety.

JUST A FEW minutes reflection will reveal that there are multiple and varied sources of scary news and information that could have emotional impact for children. Much of it exists in the background of our routines, and we adults tune it out. While eating at a pizza parlor one afternoon, my son turned to me and asked if he could turn off the TV that was over the table. I hadn't noticed it was there! We turned it off and ate in peace.

Unfortunately, many sources of scary news cannot simply be turned off. But looking at the environment with heightened awareness and sensitivity to your children's viewpoint will help you better understand what they have to deal with daily. Understanding this much will take you closer to seeing how to protect your children and how to help them see the world from a more balanced point of view. Your efforts to keep joy in your children's lives will be so much more effective and rewarding if you understand more clearly the forces at work against you.

1 National Institute of Mental Health, Depression in Children and Adolescents, A Fact sheet for Physicians publication no 00-4744, September 2000 http://www.nimh.nih.gov/publicat/ depchildresfact.cfm
2 National Institute of Mental Health, Suicide Facts, December 2003 http://www.nimh.nih.gov/research/suifact.cfm
3 Simon and Schuster, 2001

Chapter 2

Protecting Young Minds

Shield children from the harsher realities of life during the vulnerable developing years of childhood.

Protecting children from the dangers of oncoming cars is unequivocal. We understand clearly what the results will be if we don't. Shielding children from the harsh realities of the adult world is just as critical. If you want to teach children the skills to survive and flourish in a frightening world, the skills discussed in this book, you must provide a safe environment for learning.

Consider the example of infants eating solid foods. Visible and obvious signs indicate that infants cannot tolerate solid food. Infants do not have a chew and swallow reflex; they have no teeth, and they can't sit up to eat. If we give them solid food anyway, a protrusion reflex makes their tongues push food out of their mouths. Other indications are not so clearly visible. Infants' digestive systems are immature and do not have the enzymes to handle solids; their stomachs hold only small amounts of liquid. Ignoring physiological cues and giving solid food to infants too soon can result in discomfort for the baby and more serious consequences. All parents want their children to be able to eat adult food with success and enjoyment, but there is work to be done in gradual stages to reach that goal.

Robbing children of their innocence and letting them try to digest the complex and ugly issues that make the world a scary place before they are ready also gain them no advantage. Many obvious signs tell us this is not how things are meant to happen, and less obvious ones, such as brain physiology, we are learning more about.

Michael Medved and Diane Medved, Ph.D. point out the problems of exposing children too early to frightening adult information in their book, *Saving Childhood: Protecting Our Children from the National Assault on Innocence*[1]: "That kids don't run screaming from information overload is a miracle in itself. Adding scary possibilities that are not reality for them increases the burdens of their development, injecting fear, worry, paranoia, guilt, anger and pessimism to the other integrative tasks they face."

Our primary purpose is to protect the innocent and vulnerable lives placed in our care. After helping my daughter with something she found difficult one day, she turned to me with a huge smile of relief and said, "It's a good thing that grown-ups are here to help children!"

Developmental Cues

Why is early childhood the most critical and the most vulnerable time of life; why is it so important to protect children from frightening world events and spare them the vivid details? Child development experts describe the many stages all children must go through to reach physical, psychological, and emotional maturity. If you observe children of different ages, you will see that two-year-olds have different challenges and a different understanding of the world than do eight-year-olds. Toddlers are involved in the physical challenges of walking and manipulating objects. Eight-year-olds are busy with friends and the complexities of social behavior. Two-year-olds are just figuring out that they are independent; eight-year-olds are discovering what their personal skills and abilities are.

When young children are vulnerable and open to every new piece of information, exposure to violent, sordid, emotionally charged events will cause permanent and significant changes in their brain and emotional development.

Without studying developmental experts like Piaget and Erikson, parents respond to developmental cues every day. You decide when your child is ready to use the toilet, help set the table, ride a bike without training wheels, sleep away from home, answer the telephone, or mow the lawn. However, responding to visible signs of readiness, like the ability to reach the table and carry a plate, can be easier than perceiving and understanding the subtle cues of emotional and cognitive development. Like the infant's digestive system, brain physiology is hidden from view.

How do scary news and the violent realities of the world affect young minds? *When young children are vulnerable and open to every new piece of information, exposure to violent, sordid, emotionally charged events will cause permanent and significant changes in their brain and emotional development.*

Experience and the Brain

This is not just another unsubstantiated warning created to worry already-worried parents. There is a definite sequence and pattern to human brain growth and development; infants don't become happy, healthy three-year-olds automatically. The sequence of brain development is genetically programmed into one hundred billion neurons that come packaged within the human newborn; however, it is the child's *experiences* that determine how or even if, brain development takes place. The experiences growing children have will determine what their adult brains are capable of. As stated in *The Secret Life of the Brain*[2]: "The adult brain cannot be considered in isolation from the brain of the child and adolescent."

You may know that extreme neglect and abuse in infants hinders brain development, causing lifelong developmental handicaps. Children who receive barely enough care to meet basic needs for the first several years of life experience significant and extreme conditions that will clearly, in light of our current knowledge of brain development, have long-lasting consequences. Basic needs *must* be met first, as Abraham Maslow described. In his hierarchy of needs, the most basic needs are physiological, such as air, food, water, and shelter. The next level of needs is safety.

What about the average young child who is not suffering from deprivation of basic needs and who feels safe from immediate threats—children like yours and mine? How much is learned and absorbed from the interactions that occur hundreds of times a day?

We used to believe that the different brain functions were isolated in specialized areas, and if we could just understand all the functions and compartments well enough, we could take apart the brain like a complex jigsaw puzzle. Each piece would have its own assignment, or duty to perform. But now we realize that the *connections among* all the areas of the brain and the communication that takes place within and along all those pathways are even more important than the individual pieces. Like a component stereo system, nothing works right without the proper wiring.

Children don't just imitate what they see, they learn and change with every experience; their brains grow new connections and reinforce existing pathways based on their experience. Scientists refer to this as the brain's plasticity.

Fortunately, our brains can adapt and change even into old age, but childhood is the time when most connections are made. Like a young sapling, the main branches that will support later growth are formed during the rapid growing years of youth. These branches also undergo a selective pruning process during the formative years.

But how does all this wiring and growing and connecting happen? If *experience* shapes neuropathways, what is it within each experience that determines the shape it becomes?

The answer is *emotion*.

While young children are building their adult brains with each experience, they are also creating their heart's ability to love, to be empathetic, to nurture, to be intimate, to trust, to perceive and to respond to emotional cues and form a sense of their emotional self. Dr. T. Berry Brazelton says, "Emotions are actually the internal architects, conductors or organizers of our minds."[3] With each experience hearts and minds are formed together.

Emotions as Organizers

As early as the first birthday, babies begin to understand that two minds can share feelings and intentions: they will look where another person is pointing, and they will judge situations by observing the behavior of others. One particularly revealing study showed that if a one-year-old watches his mother open two boxes and look disgusted with the contents of one but delighted with the contents of the other, he will shun the first box and eagerly reach into the second.[4]

The ability to read facial expressions without verbal communication is culturally universal. What's more, we react to other people's expressions involuntarily within our body's nervous system in ways our conscious mind is unaware of, with changes in heart rate, blood pressure, and perspiration.

Even very young children pick up emotional cues from their environment; they respond within their brains and nervous systems even if we don't see a measurable outward response. This means that if very young, nonverbal child was watching the TV screen and witnessed the repeated close-ups of people reacting with shock, horror, grief and terror as the twin towers of New York City fell, responses in his nervous system shaped his neural pathways forever.

Emotions organize our memories, too. Memories with emotional significance for us are stored in different areas of the brain than memories that do not have emotions attached.[5] September 11, 2001, is a date that most Americans will remember with clarity and emotion. The kind and degree of emotion experienced on that day vary, but the memories have a strong emotional overlay and are encoded in our brains differently from other significant dates without such strong emotional meaning, such as July 4, 1776.

Shaping Neural Pathways

The physical and chemical reactions that occur with emotions are collectively called "the stress response," which is significant in numerous fields of scientific study, such as medicine, psychology, and psychiatry. Researchers in all fields agree that early childhood experience can be the key to variations found in the adult stress response.[6] For instance, repeated emotional trauma in childhood excessively stimulates the emotional memory pathway. Because it has been zapped so many times it is left raw and sensitive, like an open wound. The adult with this wounded pathway may experience a maximized stress reaction to a relatively minor stressor, but never realize its connection to the childhood experience.

I have pointed out that the brain has the property of plasticity and has the ability to change and adapt. Science has recorded amazing adaptive responses in individuals who have suffered significant emotional and physical trauma to the brain. I'm not suggesting that every shock to the system is a crippling blow. It is not useful for parents to look at every emotional event as the cause of another adult handicap, just as a bag of chips or a slice of chocolate cake does not destroy the chances for a healthy body. Most important to consider is the steady emotional diet we are feeding our children.

Even in the most protected child's life there will be disturbing and difficult events to deal with: grandparents and pets die, a best friend moves away, a loved one battles a chronic disease. These are opportunities for growth and

If we want to raise loving, caring, joyful children, they need to see loving behavior, they need to observe people caring for one another, and they need to experience joy.

learning that must be faced. Research has also shown that a loving, supportive environment can mitigate a lot of the damage caused by emotional trauma. Any loving parent or child of loving parents will testify to this truth. But why *add* tragedy and trauma that has little or nothing to do with your child's immediate life experience?

"Shielding your child's innocence isn't fruitless or hopeless or overprotective. What it really is, is responsible parenting, and the more the toxic culture is kept away from your child, the more her mind will prosper," says Jay Gordon, M.D., author of *Brighter Baby.*

Our children are constantly watching us and observing others to figure out how this world works; their hearts and minds are tirelessly taking notes during every interaction. If we want to raise loving, caring, joyful children, they need to see loving behavior, they need to observe people caring for one another, and they need to experience joy. As children take in each situation and experience, they will use it to shape their neural pathways and their future. The experience of compassion, cooperation, gentle nurturing, and unconditional loving will actually shape their brains' growth and function, giving it the mental muscle to eventually cope with the harsher side of human behavior.

Mental Muscle or Emotional Baggage

When I hear parents discuss and compare their children's ability to "handle" exposure to emotionally charged events, I know it's naiveté and not a conscious desire to harm. But let's look at it logically. The ability of a five-year-old to watch the horrors on the evening news and sleep without nightmares does not mean she is at the head of her class. Hearing about the sexual exploits of politicians does not prepare a seven-year-old to be a conscientious voter. Seeing the devastation and death in the aftermath of an earthquake does not give any child the ability to survive a natural disaster.

There is a prevailing attitude in our culture today that information equals preparation. We think that if enough information is disseminated, we will be prepared for any problem and we can prevent all kinds of personal and societal disasters. Because of our fears for our children and their future, there is a well intentioned, but over zealous attempt to load children up with any information that might keep them out of trouble down the road. But it doesn't work. Information alone is not going to steer children away from trouble or insure they will make the right choices. Too much information that has emotional impact will do damage that cannot be reversed.

Recently there has been an ad campaign in my city aimed at "educating" the public about child abuse. Huge billboards are used to shock unsuspecting commuters as they drive; the signs are designed to communicate horrifying ways of torturing children and can't be avoided. When I saw one showing a red-hot burner on a stove with the words, "Stoves should only be used for cooking dinner, prevent child abuse," I felt nauseated at the image it implied. I waited, hoping my young children wouldn't see it as we drove by.

It was the next time we passed one of those billboards, as my stomach clenched up, that my nine-year-old asked what it meant. I explained as gently as I could, but I knew he was feeling an emotional shock that would be part of his memory forever, and it made me angry to know that it was completely unnecessary. The knowledge that some adults are capable of extreme cruelty to children did nothing to help him and served only to add more fear to his job of growing up.

It is not realistic to cocoon children in protective bubbles where they will never know the darker side of life. But we can actively shield our children from unhealthy emotional baggage that adds nothing to their growth and development and more than likely does them harm.

Suggestions

As you make decisions about what your children are exposed to and what you will shield them from, ask these questions:

1. Is this information unavoidable?
2. Is this information necessary?
3. Does this information offer an opportunity for growth and deeper understanding in any way?
4. Are there signs that my child is ready for this information? (Have they asked relevant questions? Do they exhibit understanding of related concepts?)

In the billboard example, the answers to questions 2, 3 and 4 were no, but the answer to question 1 was also no. So I did what I could to be truthful, minimize the impact, and reassure my son that he is safe and loved.

If scary news is not necessary, does not offer opportunity for growth, and your children do not appear to be ready to deal with it, then it should be avoided until at least one of these conditions changes.

Even if they appear ready to handle sensitive information, if it is not necessary for their direct experience and it doesn't seem to offer an opportunity to deepen awareness or understanding, there is no reason to put it before them now. Wait until such information is needed.

If information is unavoidable and necessary because it is a part of a child's direct experience, then it can also become an opportunity for growth.

These are the times when you can really help your child build emotional muscle that will help down the road. Your knowledge of your child and any signs of readiness or developmental cues should determine what you tell and how you tell it.

My children's friends experienced an extremely frightening situation when their mother unexpectedly collapsed while fixing dinner. She did not respond to their cries, and their father was not home and was unreachable. In their panic, the children couldn't make the phone work and ran outside. Fortunately, a friendly neighbor was walking by at that moment and was able to help. My children saw the ambulance take their friends' mother to the hospital, and they heard all the scary details of the story.

This event awakened all sorts of fears in my children and me. We then talked about emergency situations and what children can do if an adult is sick or hurt. I gave them permission to do things they wouldn't normally do without permission, such as leaving the house, crossing the street and going to a neighbor, using the phone, and interrupting their father at work. Talking about the possibilities and reassuring them that they have skills to cope with unexpected situations helped us all to feel more prepared to take action, even though it would be very scary. They gained emotional muscle through that experience.

When sharing information, keep in mind your children's developmental stages.

When impending war with Iraq was the prominent news story, we shared information with our children about the situation because it was unavoidable and necessary in their daily experience. It was also an opportunity for learning and the two older children were ready to understand the information. For younger siblings scary information is often unavoidable because older members of the family talk about it. But my six-year-old, ten-year-old, and fourteen-year-old are in different developmental stages and have varying abilities to understand complex issues. So in addition to general family discussion I spoke with each child, sharing a different level of information suited to each child's age and needs.

SCARY NEWS DOES NOT slow down and watch out for children playing. Our job as parents is to keep our children safe and feeling secure while they gradually learn to cope with the complex and sometimes grim realities of adulthood. Just as we stand between our children and the deadly traffic on a busy street, we must protect our children from the damaging effects of scary news until they have gained the skills to successfully integrate them into their hearts and minds.

1 HarperCollins, 1998

2 The Dana Press and Joseph Henry Press, 2001

3 Newsweek special edition Fall/Winter 2000 "Your Child"

4 Newsweek special edition Fall/Winter 2000 "Your Child"

5 The Secret Life of the Brain, by Richard Restak, M.D., a co-publication of The Dana Press and Joseph Henry Press, pgs 115

6 as above pg 116

Chapter 3

Home is a Haven

*Create a peaceful and safe home where joy and
optimism can thrive.*

A front-page picture ten inches high of a young woman's
tear-streaked face who has lost her child to a random bullet.
A ten-second news teaser saying "The BIG one may be closer
than you think; is your home earthquake safe? We'll tell you
at ten." These kinds of messages are designed to elicit fear
and paint a picture that the world is very unsafe. But the
message children hear is that the world is unsafe and even
grown-ups can't do anything about it.

The World is Unsafe

It is commonplace to see headlines about devastating forest
fires burning through neighborhoods, tornados ripping up
houses, violent assaults, shootings, plane crashes. Although

you may understand that there is no immediate danger to your family, don't underestimate how these stories can affect your children. Scary events and the awful details of the lives lost and the families torn apart can dwell in the minds of children and stir up anxiety and fear beyond what adults

Your home should be a safe haven for everyone in the family, a place of peace where everyone can breathe easier.

would consider realistic. Using their active, creative imaginations, children will also embellish the stories with their own details, taking their general feeling of anxiety and transforming it into fear for themselves or for loved ones.

I learned too late that my son had spent many days in fear because he believed a good friend was in danger. He had heard part of a news story about a sniper and people being hurt and killed. Because he didn't understand where the events were happening, he thought his friend was in danger while he walked to school. When I found out, I reassured him and also told him (again) that he could always check things out with his father and me if for any reason he was fearful. I'll always wish that I had known and had been able to save him from those fearful hours; better yet, I wish he had never heard the story.

Take measures to limit your children's exposure to scary news and violent events. Create an environment of safety and security in your home where your children feel protected from the outside world. They should be able to play with happy security and let down the emotional guards they have when they are away from home. Your home should be a safe haven for everyone in the family, a place of peace where everyone can breathe easier.

Home Sweet Home

Many people don't consciously think about what their home environment is teaching their children. But children's surroundings while they grow up will greatly influence the kinds of homes they create when they are on their own. Your example and your efforts now will largely determine how your children view the entire concept of home. By creating an atmosphere of peace and security in your home you are surrounding your children with a nurturing setting for their childhood and you are teaching them that they can control their environment and choose what kind of home they want for themselves and their family.

Parents may not be able to control all the sources of information their children have access to, but they certainly shouldn't give up control in their own homes.

I read an article in the March 31, 2003, edition of the *Napa Valley Register* about how children may react to news of the war in Iraq. A large picture that accompanied the article showed a refugee holding a child while walking past a military tank. The caption said, "Parents can be a major influence, experts say, in how their children see war, but they cannot control when and where children will be exposed to images like this."

I disagree. Parents may not be able to control *all* the sources of information their children have access to, but they certainly shouldn't give up control in their own homes. Home is the most important place to take control and create a loving and safe environment.

∞

Ten minutes of news may lead to ten times as much explaining, comforting, and damage control. It's not worth it.

∞

Suggestions for Limiting Children's Exposure to Scary News

If you want to listen to news, do so after the children are in bed or at school.

Your hand cannot move fast enough to change the channel or shut it off when the gory pictures flash on the screen. Ten minutes of news may lead to ten times as much explaining, comforting, and damage control. It's not worth it.

If you keep the radio on in the car or at home, remember that the children are listening to every

**news flash and talk show topic with you. Play tapes
and CDs instead.**

Too often I have been in the car with my kids and have
turned on the radio to listen to music or to get the traffic
report, and an R-rated news headline is announced with
ugly details that spew out faster than I can get my hand to
the dial. My children always hear it and ask questions or
sit in tense silence until I say something. Now I don't turn
on the radio because I have no idea what will come over
the air next.

**Don't leave magazines and newspapers around for
young readers to browse through. If you share the
comics or the ads, take them out and keep adult's
reading material separate.**

Newspapers are actually a better source for information
about current events than TV news shows, but the front-page
headlines are still full of gore, scandal, disaster and death.
Older children may need the newspaper for schoolwork and
other projects, but consider it also R-rated, and always carefully monitor what they read.

**Be assertive with neighbors and friends who want to
talk about gory details when the children are present.
Say, "Let's talk about this later when we are alone."**

After a young neighbor died suddenly, I was surprised how
many times people wanted to talk about it while my children
were present. I didn't want to shield my children from the
shared grief and shock everyone was experiencing, but

I didn't think it was helpful for them to hear the details of how, when, why, and where this event happened and sensitive topics like autopsy reports and medical details.

If you want your older children to watch an informative program that could be scary or disturbing, always preview it first and watch together.

I was very glad I took the time to preview a special show about rebuilding on the site of the twin towers in New York City. When I watched it with my children, we had a very valuable discussion about the complex process of cleanup and repair and the incredibly sensitive and difficult decisions that will have to be made about the future of that site. I believe it really helped us turn our thoughts away from the painful past event and to the real issue of how to move on.

Be involved with your children's school and request the opportunity to preview materials that deal with scary news events or negative information.

Be very aware that media use in schools has become widespread. Some schools have news programs presented every day. Most public schools have also bought into the myth that information is preparation for young children. My four-year old neighbor was telling me that at his school he was learning how bad smoking is. Both his parents are chronic smokers. The information may be true, but it is not helping him understand his world better, it is not helping him feel secure at home, and it simply adds anxiety that he has no power to resolve.

Look for any opportunity to share positive stories that relate to scary news, such as acts of kindness and selflessness, the generosity of strangers, and examples of cooperation among service providers.

When your children bring home stories about tragic events or something happens close to home, always point out who helped the situation and how things were resolved. My son once remarked that whenever he heard a siren, he thought about someone being hurt. I encouraged him to remind himself that the siren means there are people helping and someone is being taken care of.

Watch your conversations with your spouse or adult friends. Make a habit of not discussing adult topics when the children are present.

Has your spouse ever walked in the door, eager to tell about something that happened during the day, and you try to talk in vague metaphors or a strange kind of code because the children are present and listening? Better to just reserve a little time in another room to unburden the activities of the day if they're not for general audiences.

Be alert to topics discussed by your children's friends. Establish guidelines for what you consider appropriate and stick to them.

My older children have learned that when sordid topics come up with their friends it's really not that hard to say, "Let's talk about something else." But young children need help setting those kinds of boundaries. I needed to gently interrupt my daughter's six-year-old friend as her conversation turned to details about her sister's boyfriend going to jail. I explained to her and my daughter that it was a private issue they didn't need to discuss, but they could always talk to me or the other mom if they had questions.

Suggestions for Creating a Joyful and Optimistic Environment

In a world where negativity seeps into every corner of our lives and whatever is gross, weird, or shocking is considered hip and appropriate for children, we must find ways to create a home environment that promotes positive thinking and joyful attitudes.

Use visible reminders of the people who love your children and share their lives.

Pictures of family and friends will remind you and your children of the love you share with others. Mementos of special times with friends are much better decorations than designer items; they decorate your home with love and joy.

Try to carve out an area that is specifically for the children.

If you have enough space to dedicate an entire room for a play area or have a private bedroom for each child, that's great. But if not, use the space you have and give up some area to the children. Let them know they are part owners of your home, not unwelcome boarders who take up valuable room. We have never had a playroom, but for a long time I had the living room couch pulled away from the wall to create a hiding place where no grown-up could fit. My older children still talk fondly of "the place behind the couch."

Invite your children's help in decorating your home, and allow them to choose things that they find inspiring.

I'm not suggesting scattering toys and cartoon characters all over the house, but let them discover what they like. If their only choices come from the toy aisle, they will miss opportunities for self-discovery. You don't have to let the kids decide which couch to buy, but you can include them in the process. Let them make small decisions that are temporary and can be changed, like what centerpiece to use on the table, or which picture to hang over the mantel, or which shower curtain to put in the bathroom.

Help your children make their room a special, personal place.

Most adults like to have their rooms be retreats from the world. Children like to have retreats too. Their rooms should definitely be more than storerooms for toys. Many decorator magazines emphasize making a child's room a playground or a miniature amusement park. I think children get enough stimulation and amusement elsewhere, so their rooms should be relaxing and peaceful. Most important is to make it a place *they* think is special.

There is strong merchandising pressure to surround children with images of TV or comic book characters. But there is more to your child's personality than a love of Pokemon. Help them to dig deeper and express something more personal. Ask them what they think is beautiful; what makes them feel good. When they are upset, what kind of place would they like to run away to? Remember to help your children discover their inner spirit by expressing it in their space.

When my son was planning his little room, he first considered painting it black and red, because he is fascinated with Spiderman. But after more discussion and encouragement, he came up with a plan to make it look like a forest meadow. His strong connection to nature is what he was able to express, and it makes his room uniquely his. It was a fun and inspiring project that he has never regretted. He loves his retreat and he still has his Spiderman toys.

When children share a room, it is still possible to let them express their unique personalities. Help them find a way, and don't worry about breaking decorating rules.

Consider very, very carefully before putting a TV in your child's room.

There are so many reasons why putting a TV in a child's bedroom is such a bad idea that entire books have been written on the subject. I will just emphasize that putting a TV in your child's bedroom is completely counter to most of the goals this book is addressing. TV allows too many opportunities to violate the safe and secure environment you are trying so hard to create. Resolve viewing conflicts in other ways, and keep the TV in the main area of the house where you have control. Don't give in to the whining and pleading: and remember that a TV is not a toy.

Bring nature indoors

The beauty of the natural world is a wonderful way to make your home more peaceful and uplifting. There are many ways to bring nature into your home with pictures, plants, and fabric. Children love to bring rocks, shells, feathers, pinecones, flowers and leaves home to admire and share, but we often don't know what to do with the treasures after we empty our pockets. Try creating a nature display dedicated to these special collections. We have a nature tray in our home that we use to keep our wonderful discoveries together and when it gets full we discard old things to make room for new.

Try to declutter and beautify your home.

Ideally, everything you look at as you gaze around your home should be something you enjoy seeing or using. Fill your home with things you think are beautiful, and then try to keep it neat and clean so you can enjoy the surroundings. Teach your children to respect the things you own and to treat them with care. Everything should be comfortable and accessible, but you'll find it so much more enjoyable if it is orderly, too. Provide practical storage for the children to use so that "clean up your room" is not an impossible task.

Teach your children to pay attention to their surroundings and to listen to their feelings.

Although a difficult concept to articulate, I think it is important to teach children that it is possible to feel the atmosphere of a place on an inner level. You can substitute your own word here, but places can give off a kind of aura, energy, vibration, atmosphere, or ... In some places it is very subtle and in others it is pretty obvious, even to less sensitive people. One example is a cathedral. Most people whisper in a cathedral and step softly. They can feel the years of worship that have taken place within the walls and almost hear the choir singing. There are homes that welcome you and surround you with warmth as soon as you step in the front door; there are homes that seem to push you out the door.

I think children need to recognize how a place feels to them, to pay attention to their inner sense and practice using and learning to trust it. Such recognition can be a valuable tool. There may come a time when some thing or some place doesn't

Environment can be much stronger than the most determined will power.

"feel" right, and this intuitive sense will guide them in making decisions or choices. It may help keep them from harm, or it may simply help them choose their first apartments.

ENVIRONMENT CAN BE much stronger than the most determined will power. In this modern world where scary news is so prevalent, it's absolutely necessary to create a fortress of beauty, hope, and peace where we can relax and remind ourselves that these things are a reality, too. Consciously choose to surround yourself and your children with more than love; give yourself visible reminders of the power of beauty and harmony in the world. Choose to make peace and beauty a priority at home, and they will give you strength.

Chapter 4

The Importance of Friends

Choose true friends who share strength, courage and optimism.

One rainy gray autumn morning I was walking through my neighborhood, a black umbrella shielding me from the cold drizzle. The overcast sky and the black umbrella blocked out any visible ray of sunshine. The trees were at their peak of fall color, and as I walked beneath the most brilliant ones I realized that the light *under* the trees was bright and warm and gave a glow to everything nearby. Somehow, the brilliant color of the leaves captured more light than was otherwise visible on such a day; the tree glowed with a radiance that

Nothing can change our attitude faster than being in the presence of others with negative attitudes.

True friends are heroes, offering their lives in joyful service, comforting, teaching, supporting, encouraging, and honestly loving.

appeared to come more from within than from without. It was the opposite of the shadow I had expected, filling me with awe and an inner warmth that lasted a long time.

Some people are like those trees, glowing with an inner light. I have been lucky enough to know many of them. One of the strongest weapons we have against fear and the negative influences that run rampant in our culture is the joy of good company. The opposite is just as true: Nothing can change our attitude faster than being in the presence of others with negative attitudes.

Choosing Friends

The ability to choose good friends is one of the most important skills our children can learn to help them experience joy and keep fear at bay. True friends are heroes, offering their lives in joyful service, comforting, teaching, supporting, encouraging, and honestly loving. Be sure your children have friends who inspire them and guide them in positive directions, whether they are young playmates or adults whom your children spend time with.

If you want to see whether a friend is good for your children, look at how your children act in their friend's presence:

- What do the children talk about when they get together?
- How do they settle differences?
- Does the friendship seem to be balanced and reciprocal?
- Does the friend include others in play, or shut out newcomers?
- Does the friend help your children think about new options and new directions, or insist on "how it's always been done"?
- Are others allowed to express ideas and opinions without put-downs or negative comments?
- Is the friend basically hopeful and happy and a positive influence on others?

A Friend's Influence

In my children I have noticed different reactions to different friends' influence. Sam played frequently with my older son, and they seemed to have common interests and a lot to talk about. Sam also had a younger brother who played with my younger son, and that was a convenient arrangement for all four boys. However, after a while it was clear that my younger son and Sam did not get along. My son complained about Sam's mean attitude and his teasing. My older son's behavior became an issue, also, and I tried several tactics to solve the problem. I spoke with all the boys and the other mother. I separated the younger boys from the older boys to discourage the sibling rivalry.

But it slowly became apparent that Sam bullied his younger brother with sarcasm and subtle intimidation, which his brother accepted as normal. Although Sam was genuinely fond of my older son and was a pleasant companion when the younger brothers were not around, his attitude toward his sibling extended to all little brothers and influenced my older son's attitude negatively.

The two older boys would ridicule the younger boys' imaginative play and belittle any contributions they had toward conversation until my younger son would dissolve into tears or explode with anger. Sam would take the lead, and my older son had a difficult time not joining in even though Sam's behavior was rude and unacceptable by our family standards.

We talked about the problem as a family, and we discussed the fact that Sam's family life was difficult and our home was a peaceful haven for him. However, we were not willing to compromise that peace because of one visitor. My son recognized and took responsibility for his behavior, but admitted it was difficult to stand up to Sam's strong personality and his attitude that little brothers were pests to tease and ridicule. We agreed to all work together to communicate to Sam that he was welcome, but his attitude toward the younger boys would not be tolerated.

It wasn't long before Sam grew tired of my watchful eye and the constant reminders that he was expected to follow our house rules. He stopped coming around so much, and the boys grew apart although they remained friends. Sadly, his little brother also took on the sarcastic, hurtful behavior and ended his friendship with my younger son. We all learned a great deal about evaluating friendship and listening to our inner experience to guide our decisions.

Our experience with Sam was a strong contrast to our experience with another young boy. Michael also became friends with my older son, and he, too, had young siblings. Michael's friendship is strong with my older son, but he is friendly and considerate toward my younger son and my daughter, too. Our entire family is happy and relaxed when he is in our home; and when I announce that Michael is coming for a visit, both brothers are thrilled to hear the news. We all value our experience with Michael, and we recognize that he is a positive companion for all of us.

Sometimes your children may be stronger in talents or abilities than their friends. Your children may be a good example and inspire a friend to work harder on something they find difficult. If the friendship is balanced overall this arrangement can work well

Your friendships will have a huge impact on your children

for everyone. But if *all* your children's friends look up to them for inspiration without giving any in return, there may be little challenge to grow. Encourage friendships that challenge your children and inspire them to experience new possibilities within themselves, also.

Friends and Scary News

My best friend was on vacation away from home when she heard about the horrific events of Sept. 11. She tried to continue with her plans but came home early, not because of fear, but because she didn't feel right being away from friends. When scary news hits the headlines, we usually think of our friends, after we consider the safety of our family. We will contact our friends to be comforted and reassured and offer them the same. Your children may have a need to connect with their friends when they are anxious, too. When my son heard of a large explosion and fire in Texas, he wanted to call and talk with his friend who lives there even though he understood his friend was not in danger. I overhear my children discussing scary news events with their friends, just as we do with ours. Hearing the voice of a friend can keep our heart open and fear away. We can help our children have strong and lasting friendships if we allow them to follow their heart and express their feelings of friendship in their unique way.

Do not protect yourself by a fence, but rather by your friends.
(Czech Proverb)

Suggestions

Set an example by choosing your friends carefully, and talk to your children about the qualities you value in your friends.

Some parents may worry that consciously selecting friends in this way teaches children to be critical or narrow minded. I am not suggesting you look for friends for yourself or your children who think the same as you, or those who are successful in a worldly way, or those who can help you meet the "right" people and have impressive status or prestige. After spending time with good friends, my children and I often talk about how we feel when we are with these special people, what we learn from them, and why we cherish the opportunities we have to be with them. Our hearts seem to be bigger after each encounter.

Look at your child's behavior, not your personal preferences, as a barometer.

Ask yourself, "Is this friendship helping my child to move toward expansion and love?" Gently guide your children toward positive influences, and be prepared to give them specific reasons why you have concerns if you believe a change is needed.

Include your children in your acts of friendship and let them learn from your example.

Your friendships will have a huge impact on your children, and you should be aware that they could learn a great deal from your example. One morning I got a call from a dear friend who was in tears because her cat had been killed. I wanted to help her, but my husband was not available and there was no one to watch my children. After some thought I realized that I should include the children and let them experience what it is like to support a friend during an emotional time. My friend was grateful for their presence, and my children showed me what good friends they can be.

Encourage your children to listen to their inner guidance about the company they keep.

Sometimes my children are uncomfortable with other children and I can't figure out why. I've had to remind myself that I need to respect their feelings and their individuality. As parents we can teach our children social graces and gently encourage them if they are shy or hesitant about new friends. We can arrange time together and provide an environment for playing and sharing interests so friendships can blossom. But we can't force friendship on our children; it's an individual choice.

Encourage your child's loving gestures toward friends.

Most children get very excited about doing things or making things for their friends. It is so important to encourage and support those impulses, however trivial they seem. This is how children learn what it feels like to open their hearts and include others in their world. I remember my daughter writing a secret message for her friend who was out of town. With lots of giggling and anticipation of her return, we crept over to her friend's house and left the message. We both had fun.

One friend won't meet every need.

Some of us have a wide circle of friends, and some feel happy with just a few. Children often passionately cling to one close buddy to the exclusion of other potential friends. Encourage a variety of friends, and reassure your children that one person will not meet every need. My older son finds it interesting that three friends share his three favorite interests individually.

Some friends will not be forever.

Although some friends may stick with us from kindergarten to college and beyond, many friends will come into our lives for shorter periods. Help your children to understand that a friendship that fades away is not a failure. Every friendship is a gift to be treasured while it's here and treasured as a special memory when we (or they) have moved on.

BY CHOOSING UPLIFTING, positive companions, your children will learn to appreciate others and will expand their awareness to include all kinds of people. Ultimately, they will attract lifelong friends who will light their way in times of darkness and confusion and be there with loving support when you cannot.

Chapter 5

Our Need for Comfort

Comfort ourselves and others in times of need.

Despite our best efforts to protect our children from scary news and make them feel safe, at times they will experience fear and will need comforting. When we provide comfort we teach valuable skills they will use to comfort themselves when we are not available. To be able to seek and find comfort when we need it is a basic survival skill; seeking comfort is an acknowledgment of pain and the first step toward healing. If we find no comfort for our pain, we just have to live with it, or bury it, or try to get rid of it— usually by dumping it on someone else. The world can be very scary when there is no comfort to be found.

The power of a parent's presence is greater than any technique or training

The Power of Presence

Of all the comforting techniques available, the best tool parents have is their *presence*. The power of a parent's presence is greater than any technique or training and gives children a shield, a source of strength, a familiar face as well as a role model for coping with all kinds of stressful situations.

In the frantic pace kept by today's families, children are often without their parents for long periods. Even very young children may have to cope with their fears from early morning until bedtime without an opportunity to express what they are feeling and without their parents' comforting presence. During times of stress especially, regardless of the cause of the anxiety, being together can give everyone in the family a sense of security and even erase the fears that young children may be struggling with.

When my daughter was very little and just beginning to talk, she seemed to have a fascination with the idea of mommies, daddies, and babies. In her mind, everyone and everything fit into one of those three categories. Like the story of the three bears, she would put things or people into their proper category by size. She was really pleased when she had three sizes of anything and she could line them up as big daddy, medium mommy, and little baby. She would do this with sticks and rocks while playing outside, she would do it with her toys, and she would even do it with silverware at the dining room table. If three sizes weren't available, she would use two and designate the big one as either mommy or daddy, depending on its characteristics or her mood at the time.

As she grew a bit older, she added siblings to the picture, because she has two big brothers. She also learned that not all grown-up females were mommies and not all grown-up males were daddies. So she decided they were *like* mommies and daddies, which was the next best thing.

It was fascinating to me that, without training, this very young child seemed to have a built in understanding of a complex concept. But for her it wasn't complex. It was simple: big people take care of little people. She had complete confidence and trust that this was the way the world worked, and we did everything to reinforce her confidence.

In the chapter three, I explained that people react to emotional cues with the stress response, and that response is measurable. To understand the long-term effects of stress, anxiety, and fear on children, studies have been done to measure the stress response in many circumstances. What these studies repeatedly prove is that even with no verbal or nonverbal comfort, the presence of a parent or an adult the child is familiar with and completely secure with will minimize the child's stress response. An adult the child does not have a secure relationship with *will not produce the same effect.*

In their book, Raising Resilient Children, Robert Brooks, Ph.D. and Sam Goldstein, Ph.D describe it this way: "Increasingly, scientific research demonstrates the importance of parent-child relationships to the development of competence and resilience. This is true not just for children facing extraordinary challenges, but for all children.... When adversity is present and effective adults are unavailable, risk for serious life problems is high."[1]

While watching a television show about animal behavior with my daughter, we saw how a mother turtle laid its eggs in the sand and return to the ocean, leaving them behind alone. The eggs hatched and the little turtles slowly made their way to the water without their mother's help. My daughter was very disturbed about this and kept asking, where was the mommy? She couldn't accept the truth that this was normal turtle behavior. She had to reassure herself and me that the mommy turtle was there

Listen to what your children say about their feelings and be honest with them about yours.

watching, but was just out of camera range. Children expect their parents to be there for them. Sadly, many have to learn not to expect it.

A myth that our culture seems to be buying into is the idea that if there is a "village" of teachers, day-care providers, babysitters, youth workers, coaches, and mentors, parents don't need to be with their children. We often view as over-protective or old fashioned to dedicating time to our children through their childhood years. Don't believe it. Whatever fearful situation your child must handle, it will not be as scary if you are there.

Follow your instincts. If you feel your child needs you near, do whatever is within your power to make it happen. I know of a woman who took her teenage daughter out of school as soon as she heard about the terrorist attacks on New York and Washington D.C. Some may have thought she was overreacting, or overprotective, or that she didn't trust the school to handle the situation; but she knew her daughter would feel the same shock and fear she was experiencing. So she took her daughter home where she could control the information her daughter was being given, she could explain the situation in her own way, and, most important, she could look into her daughter's eyes and provide a mother's loving, comforting presence. I doubt she'll ever regret her decision.

The Power of Routine

The more chaos there is in the world, the more the simple, daily routines provide comfort and security. Children especially draw comfort from familiar rituals and patterns of behavior, so whenever possible continue your family routine during times of emotional stress. Try to eat meals and get the children to bed at the regular time. Take time to read stories, take baths, and snuggle together if that's what you usually do. Whether because of a world news event or a personal family concern you may feel distracted, rushed, or simply unable to follow through with normal activities. But listen to the children when they remind you, "But we *always* do that on Wednesdays!" They are telling you they need routine to feel safe.

Read familiar stories, cook familiar foods, play familiar family games and you'll find comfort, too. Television shows may be the routine after dinner, but avoid TV when it's likely to be filled with news reports, emotional interviews, or frightening images. Pick out an old video or read out loud instead.

After the September 11 terrorist attacks, I really didn't want to take my son to soccer practice, but he expected it. After some thought, I decided it was better for him to be engaged in a familiar activity than sitting at home feeling helpless and angry. Later, I was glad we stayed with the routine because it was calming for both of us.

On the other hand, if your schedule demands more than you can handle, it may be better to change your plans. Perhaps you have a full calendar with separate activities for everyone but you would rather the family be together. Give yourself permission to follow your heart and comfort one another at home.

The Power of Touch

Have you ever put on a pair of old worn pajamas when you were upset or pulled out a soft sweater to wear when you knew it was going to be a difficult day? Humans are tactile creatures; our sense of touch is a universal way we have of calming ourselves, communicating with others, and comforting our children. We know touch has the power to reassure, soothe, and even heal. Touch alone can lower blood pressure and heart rate, change breathing patterns, and decrease muscle tension.

Praying with children can be a great source of comfort, inspiration, peace, and gratitude, taking many forms that will change and develop as children grow.

When we cuddle under a soft blanket or put on a favorite old shirt, we are showing our children one way they can comfort themselves in times of stress. It may soothe you and your children to brush their hair or rub their feet during a time of tension and worry. Rocking together or giving a backrub is another way to provide comfort and reassurance. If your children are not receptive to a hug or they are too big to sit on your lap, an alternative such as a warm bath, a soft robe, or a comfy spot on the couch can work just as well.

Don't underestimate what a simple hand squeeze or pat on the back can communicate. When my son was quite young and became very upset at the park one afternoon, I firmly held his hand as we walked the three blocks toward home. Although he didn't want to hold my hand, he was so emotional that I wouldn't let go because I knew he might run away from me. As we walked, I didn't try to talk to him, but I gave his hand three quick squeezes. I took a few more steps and squeezed his hand three times again. He angrily asked me what I was doing. I told him that I was saying "I—love—you" with my hand. He took both hands and tried to squeeze mine with all his strength. I said, "I bet that means you're mad at me." He nodded. Before we reached home, I felt three squeezes come from his hand, and we were both a lot calmer. Since that day three squeezes have meant "I—love—you"; we use the signal frequently.

The measures we use to comfort our children will change as they grow. We need to consider developmental needs, as well as our children's unique personalities and the circumstances when we decide how best to comfort. We also must be ready to adapt if something doesn't work.

Suggestions

Support your children's need for love objects

Many children form strong attachments to favorite blankets or stuffed animals that can last into the teen years. The familiar feel and smell of the beloved object can stop tears from flowing, calm hysterical sobs, and make nightmares disappear. Not every child will have a "lovey," though, even if parents encourage it. Each of my three children has had a different kind of attachment. One had a favorite blanket from infancy that will always be cherished; another has formed emotional attachments to blankets and stuffed animals on a rotating basis with equal passion; my third never seems to have a particular favorite and chooses a doll or toy to cuddle by some inexplicable system I haven't figured out yet.

I believe loveys are an important part of heart development for some children. Support your children's passion for particular comfort items with patience and understanding while you also teach and model other ways of comforting. In times of stress children will often revert to earlier habits they seemed to have outgrown, so if you put away the lovey to encourage new ways of coping, you may still want to have it accessible to pull out if needed.

Children find comfort from unseen helpers

Although some children are too down-to-earth to be attracted to the idea of unseen helpers, others find comfort through imaginary friends, guardian angels, and magical creatures like elves or fairies. They long for imaginary worlds and can see wonderful possibilities within a tiny forest of clover or the colors of a rainbow. Happy thoughts of angels hovering nearby, fairies dancing in the moonlight, or invisible companions are joys that open the heart and strengthen children for whatever may be ahead. Such joys can encourage positive thinking and imaginative play, lifting thoughts out of fear and doubt into hope and light. Be sure, however, such helpers are a natural expression of the heart and are not forced upon a child who is more comfortable in the concrete world of trucks and blocks.

Many times, as fear of the dark took hold despite my reassurances and a bright night-light, I told my children stories of beautiful guardian angels who tenderly watch over them night and day. I have always assured them of God's constant presence and love, but sometimes the idea that God would send special angels as helpers seemed to have a more personal feel in their young minds. Together we painted invisible pictures of our angels, deciding what they might wear and what they might look like; the children decided if they preferred a boy or girl angel and sometimes chose a name. Those conversations have floated away now. I am not sure how much my children remember of those talks, but they provided great deal of comfort at the time.

Talking with your children provides comfort

Talking to children about current events and frightening news may seem an obvious comfort measure; however, many parents overlook it. It's easy to assume that children have all the information they need from school and the media and wouldn't want to listen to more talk from concerned parents.

Information can certainly help clarify issues and define what is really happening. But sometimes what we forget is that talking to our children allows them to hear what our understanding is *and* gives them the chance to discuss their fears. Imparting information shouldn't be the only goal, however. Demonstrating a willingness to listen and to share concerns is just as important.

Timing is critical. Scary news can bombard us anytime, but talking about it works best when parents and children are calm and unhurried. Before bed is often a time when the house is quieter, and you may be able to talk with your children individually or together with better results than during the day. I know a woman who was raising her son alone and found he would talk to her more openly when they sat together in the dark at bedtime. So even when he was old enough to go off to bed by himself, she would often remind him that it was okay to come and talk after bedtime if he needed to. He would then come to her room and reveal his concerns without distractions or interruptions as she listened with full attention.

Bedtime may not be the best time to talk to young children about scary topics. You may find that it backfires and nobody gets much sleep! Little children often talk when they are engaged in quiet activities such as coloring or reading stories. In a relaxed and comfortable atmosphere, children often reveal what is on their minds and you can let them know you are willing to listen.

During quiet activities my children have come up with remarks that let me know scary events are on their minds long after I stopped thinking about them. "Was something the matter with Laura's heart that did make her die?" "I've never seen a real robber [my daughter's word for any bad guy] before"; "I don't know why some people want to do bad things"; "It's good I know Susie's phone number, because I could call her house if something bad happened" my children have said, that caught me by surprise and taught me always to be prepared to deal with sensitive topics.

If you are willing to stop what you are doing and answer questions as they arise, your children will be reassured that it's okay to bring up scary questions. Don't expect to take care of them all at once; be prepared to deal with the same questions, or variations on a theme, as each child processes the issue.

Listen to what your children say about their feelings and be honest with them about yours. Talking can be a way to comfort, inform, share, and work through feelings, but it shouldn't be a way to try and *change* what your children are feeling.

The Grief Recovery Institute® advises, "If your child said they were happy, you would not try to fix or alter that feeling. Therefore there is no need to fix a feeling of sadness or fear. Feelings need to be heard, not fixed. We all need to feel safe enough to talk about how we feel. Since feelings are normal and do not need to be fixed—Hear Them—Don't Fix Them."[2]

Often children are just looking for reassurance that their thoughts are not weird. They will heave a sigh of relief when you tell them it's normal to wonder about that, or you have considered the same thing yourself. I remember when a young guest in our home confessed he was scared of clowns and how pleased he was when he learned that my husband had always thought clowns were scary, too. Just the knowledge that he was not alone in his fear was obviously a relief and a comfort.

Most important, when we talk to our children about scary issues we can bring light and love into something that may otherwise live alone in the dark of fear. We can comfort our children with the knowledge that they do not have to deal with anything alone; we can always look at it and deal with it together.

Reassure your children that you have taken safety precautions in your home

When it is possible, reassure your children that safety precautions have been taken to protect the family against harm. For instance, show them your smoke detectors and other fire safety tools if they are concerned about fire. Make fire escape plans and disaster plans together so all family members are informed and prepared. As a school project my children and I made disaster packs. In preparation for a severe storm or other crisis, we put together backpacks that held emergency supplies and items appropriate for children to use. We enjoyed the process, and it gave us an opportunity to discuss each item and how it would help us in case of a power outage or evacuation.

Remember the guidelines suggested in chapter 2 and only give information that is necessary, appropriate, or you believe your child needs for comfort. You will create more anxiety if your children are told more than they can understand or are interested in knowing.

Try to resolve some of the scary news with your children

Another way to provide comfort and to start the process of healing is to help provide some resolution to the scary news. We adults have life experiences that can provide resolutions to disturbing stories. For instance, you may hear a news story about a forest fire that burned thousands of acres. You may never follow up to find out what happened, but your experience tells you that forest fires are eventually controlled and after some cleanup by fire fighters, nature starts to regrow. You know that forest fires can be devastating, but they are not unusual. You probably also understand that a lot of good comes from forest fires and the changes that take place in the soil actually help the ecosystem. Your experience has provided your own resolution to that event.

But young children don't have the same experience and aren't able to provide resolution. A child may have scary questions that are never answered, such as, "What happened to all the animals?" "Will the fire keep burning and come to my house?" "What if they run out of water and can't put the fire out?" "Will all the trees be gone?"

With a little information and reassurance you can help your children see some resolution to scary issues and help provide a broader perspective that is less personal and threatening to them. Every issue needn't become a long lecture and detailed lesson, however, but just a little discussion can provide a lot of comfort. If you don't have the answers, you can always learn about the issue together.

Pray with your children

Prayers are intensely personal, unique, and varied as snowflakes but far more enduring. Prayer can involve complex ritual and language defined by religious doctrine or consist simply of a wordless soul call when we feel out of control or perhaps overwhelmed with joy. Praying with children can be a great source of comfort, inspiration, peace, and gratitude, taking many forms that will change and develop as children grow.

I used to lie in bed with my son when he was around two years old and we would whisper in the dark as he relaxed into sleep. Once I was looking for a way to help him let go of his toddler energy and move his mind away from all the activities of the day, so I began listing all the people who loved him, starting with his daddy and me. He immediately focused on adding to the list and thought about his grandparents and friends and even animals he knew who loved him. We had made a long list by the time he drifted off to sleep with thoughts of all those special people in his mind. For a while it was a ritual we both looked forward to, and it never failed to warm my heart and fill me with gratitude and a deep sense of blessing. It really was a prayer of thanksgiving we shared; I always think of those times as our first prayers together. My husband taught our children that one of the best ways to relax and go to sleep with positive thoughts is to pray for others, to review all their loved ones in their minds and send loving blessings to each until they fall asleep.

WHATEVER YOUR PRACTICE of prayer, your children will benefit by being included in it. They will learn to expand their awareness beyond what they can see, to connect with you in a deeper way, and to recognize and express their spiritual nature. Regardless of the words used and the rituals involved, whether solitary or communal, long or short, loud or silent, all prayers are an acknowledgment that we can't cope with life alone and we need help. We can tap into the greatest source of comfort and power in the universe if only we open our hearts and ask.

1 Contemporary Books, 2001
2 *After the Fall of the Towers,* by Russell Friedman and John W. James http://www.grief-recovery.com/Articles/after_the_fall_of_the _towers.htm

 PART II

*Help Your Children Become
Joyful and Positive*

Chapter 6

Deciding When to Defend

Discriminate when to take action and defend against a threat.

Every day we encounter messages that communicate possible threats to our safety, happiness, or well–being. To live joyfully and optimistically, we must be able to discriminate among the many threatening messages we receive. Dr. Gunnar's definition of stress mentioned in chapter 1 states that *stress exists when we perceive something as a threat and attempt to defend against it.*

Sometimes we are able to take action to defend ourselves in external and concrete ways—we hear about the dangers of carbon monoxide poisoning so we install carbon monoxide detectors in our homes, for instance. Buckling our seat belts, brushing our teeth, joining a neighborhood watch group, are all ways to protect ourselves from harm. Usually the stress involved in making a decision and taking such action is considerably less than when we feel powerless and do nothing.

When we perceive a message as threatening but feel unable to take action or defend against it, we can experience a great deal of stress in the form of anxiety, worry, and fear. National alerts regarding terrorism, "bad" economic indicators, political corruption, and environmental issues can cause anxiety but are so big and vague that we may feel a loss of control. Even if we are given the opportunity to do something specific, taking on every issue that could be threatening is overwhelming and impossible; the stress of trying would be self-destructive.

If every headline and every news event is perceived as a personal deadly threat, there is no room for normal functioning, least of all joyful participation in daily life. So we all have to make choices, whether conscious or not, about when to take action. Most adults have the ability to sort through all the scary news they encounter and decide when they will respond. However, children aren't able to discriminate between threats that are real and require action and those that are not; it is a skill they must learn.

Fight or Flight Mechanism

In many circumstances our self–defense is instinctive, without conscious thought. Our fight or flight mechanism helps us survive life–threatening situations; it's so deeply rooted that we can't turn it off even when we want to. Charles Darwin once attempted an experiment regarding his instinctive fear response. He put his face within inches of a deadly snake at the zoo, thick glass between them. With firm determination not to move if the snake struck out, he instantly jumped several feet when the snake tried to attack. It was not a conscious reaction; his conscious mind knew the glass was there, but he couldn't control his survival instinct. This instinct, while invaluable at times, becomes counterproductive and debilitating if we continually react to multiple insignificant events as serious threats or continuously react to one traumatic experience.

One day my three-year-old showed me how well I had taught her about the dangers of moving cars. I had taken the kids out for pizza and parked our van in a space that had an empty space on our right. Another car was parked opposite the empty space, its headlights pointing toward the space beside us. I got out first and opened the door on the right side of the van to let the children out. My boys stood next to the van in the empty space and waited for me to unhook their sister from her car seat. I lifted her down, put her on the ground next to her brothers, and turned to shut the door. But as soon as I set her on the ground and she saw the headlights of a car within a few feet of where she was standing, she reacted as if the car were about to run her down. She screamed and turned to me to save her.

Living joyfully is a conscious choice that will not happen without effort.

As I grabbed her and reassured her that she was safe, I could feel her heart pounding and her whole body trembling with the fight or flight fear response. I held her tightly, trying to erase her fear with my arms and hoping her memory would be of my saving her, not of putting her in harm's way.

My daughter had received the information that cars are dangerous, and she reacted to the perceived threat involuntarily. I felt some reassurance that she recognized cars as a potential danger, but the incident also gave me a deeper understanding that warnings aren't enough. Information alone does not result in preparation. My young daughter lacked the experience and maturity to realize that she *wasn't* in danger. And I hadn't anticipated her fear; my experience had told me not to be threatened by parked cars and I chose not to respond as if they were, saving myself a great deal of stress. What would happen to our daily lives if I saw every parked car as life threatening, requiring me to take action?

With time and effort, Darwin may have been able to train himself not to react to the snake behind the glass, but to what end? Protecting oneself against a deadly snake is a reasonable response. However, if Darwin were in the position of regularly encountering many varieties of snakes, he would have to learn to discriminate between the deadly ones and the harmless ones or he would be in a constant state of defensiveness and extraordinary stress.

The multiple levels of information and environmental cues we receive make the task of discrimination more complex than simply learning that some things are a threat and some things aren't, like learning which snakes are poisonous. We develop subtle layers of understanding over time. For instance, I may not always see parked cars as a threat, but I do know that a parked car *can* become a moving car. I have experienced a sudden jolt of fear while strolling past parked nonthreatening cars when one unexpectedly moves in my direction.

Although I don't want my daughter to feel threatened by every car she sees, I also don't want her to assume there is never any danger. I want her to learn to discriminate when a defense is needed and to be aware that conditions are always changing. I also want her to understand that she has choices concerning her response to threatening messages or circumstances.

Discriminating Choices

Living joyfully is a conscious choice that will not happen without effort. It takes conscious, persistent effort *not* to be victimized by the menacing, negative, and crisis laden messages that exist around us. Recognizing that you are responsible for your choices will prepare your children to face their own choices with equal responsibility.

As we process the vast amount of information and scary messages we are exposed to, much of it we can subconsciously dismiss as irrelevant (like cars parked in a parking lot). We immediately know if the issue touches our lives in a significant way or whether we have a desire to include it in our lives at this time. We know we can choose *not* to take it on or take measures to protect against it.

When the SARS virus was being discussed in the news, I had a variety of emotional reactions that related to my roles as a former nurse, a wife, a mother and even a U.S. citizen. Despite my concern and curiosity, however, I chose not to react to the news as being a personal threat. There was nothing I could do to change the situation, and the information did not directly affect my life at that time. I mentally filed the news in a "keep an eye on this" category, knowing circumstances could change.

Even when events are far beyond our control, our attitudes and actions are not.

On another day there was different news story that I also dismissed until the situation became personal and required my attention. Protesters had gathered in my city's downtown area and became violent. As the hours passed they blocked off roads and bridges and injured police. The situation became more serious as the evening wore on, but I wasn't concerned for my safety until it suddenly occurred to me that in the evening I would be attending a meeting across town. Now here was a threat I had to do something about. I examined the option of going considerably out of my way to avoid trouble and thought about the concern my family would experience if I chose to go. I decided to stay home.

In both circumstances the only thing I could control was my response. We always have the option to panic, become angry, lash out at others in frustration, or focus all available energy on the negative. But we also always have the choice to calmly make a decision and move on with a positive attitude.

Paul Foxman, Ph.D., author of The Worried Child, Recognizing Anxiety in Children and Helping Them Heal, points out: "One of the most important steps in dealing with children's worry and anxiety is to distinguish between what we can control and what we cannot control. The best way to live when bad things might happen is to focus on what we can control—namely ourselves—and let go of worry."[1]

∞

Meeting change with optimism will teach your children resilience and courage.

∞

Help your children learn to build discrimination skills and to understand that they have control over how to react to scary news. Too often we let our emotions push us into thoughtless, damaging, and cruel behavior about events we are not even a part of. The Rodney King riots are one disturbing example, and history is full of many others. Tragic events understandably provoke strong emotions, particularly fear. But even when events are far beyond our control, our attitudes and actions are not.

Taking action to help others or to initiate change, feeling compassion and sympathy, even taking measures to avoid threats and to protect ourselves are all part of being aware and alert and of making conscious choices based on love, not fear.

Choosing not to defend is important for survival.

Continually reacting to possible threats with stress and worry can lead to anxiety disorders that interfere with normal functioning. We want to help our children establish a healthy ability to *not* react defensively. Many parents have a high level of anxiety that naturally affects their children and addressing our own fears first can make a big difference for the whole family.

If you lie awake worrying about what-if scenarios that may come up in the future, remind yourself that every day is an opportunity to practice these lessons with your children, when the stakes are low. That is what childhood is for—lots of practice.

Imagine your children are preparing to attend a birthday party and they are worried about the other children being friendly, or if they'll like the food, or if they'll get hurt playing the games. You naturally reassure them and encourage them to wait and see rather than try to protect themselves against a threat that may not appear. Many lessons can be learned from this small scenario, and one is about choosing how and when to react defensively. You are helping your children build that mental file labeled "keep an eye on this" by gently telling them that a defense is not needed at this time and that they can control how they respond.

Another important lesson is showing your children how to make decisions based on love, not fear. Going to a party where there is opportunity for learning and interaction with friends, for sharing in another's happiness and expressing feelings of friendship, is a move toward expansion and joy and away from fear.

Sometimes we react with stress because conditions change and we don't want them to. Change is inevitable and is not a threat in itself. We can do our children a great service by teaching them that change is natural and is not something to fear. Our reaction to change can make the circumstances appear dreadful or promising; both reactions will affect how our children adapt. The result could be that our children hold back because of fear, or they could be ready to move ahead into a new adventure.

Meeting change with optimism will teach your children resilience and courage. Provide plenty of opportunities to deal with change while balancing their need for security and routine. Changing the furniture around, trying new foods, or taking a new route home from school are small ways to prepare for bigger changes like moving to a new town, or attending a new school, or starting a new job.

Research in brain physiology shows that new experiences create more and stronger connections among nerve cells, which occurs in young growing brains as well as in adult brains. These connections enable us to use a greater portion of our brain power to problem solve, adapt, and recall what we learned from past events. Learning to deal with change builds mental muscle for future challenges.

Despite all our efforts there is always something else to worry about or prepare our children for. But if we try to prepare our children for every eventuality with equal seriousness, we will immobilize them with anxiety and their ability to cope will be crippled. Instead, we need to focus on teaching them the ability to evaluate and discriminate information. The ability to consciously choose how and when to defend themselves will serve them in all areas of life.

When You Have to Respond to Scary News

When scary news must be dealt with, we need to answer several questions:

- What is the problem?
- What is the source of the information?
- Is the problem immediate?
- What can I do about it?
- What do those I trust say about it?

These questions may be answered immediately, or they may take much longer to work through. For example: The headline in the morning paper warns of a severe drought. If conditions don't change there will be water rationing, crops will be lost, water and food prices will escalate, fire hazard will be high, and so on. Water rationing is scheduled to begin in one week. You knew there was a problem, but now realize it is an immediate threat. You begin planning more conservation and storage of water, and you even consider leaving the area and staying with friends if it gets really bad. You can feel yourself getting tense as you consider all the possibilities.

You decide to talk with your spouse and call your friend at the water bureau for support and verification.

Young children don't have the skills to consider all these questions. They will most likely jump from the first question to the last. Where will they look for validation of such scary news? *To parents or other trusted adults.* Hearing about the drought from a friend or from a news headline, they may come to you and ask, "Will we have to move because there's no water?" Older children may consider some of the same questions you did, but reach different conclusions. Peers with little or no information may just feed their fears.

Remember that your children are watching you and learning. As you make choices about the best way to respond to scary news, they will be aware of your verbal as well as your nonverbal cues. You, in turn, must be aware of what tools you are giving them to make their own decisions.

Suggestions

Be honest about your feelings

Your children will follow your lead. Whatever the situation, your emotions will be the strongest influence on their response. If you are fearful, they will most likely know, so it will help to be honest about your feelings. However, admitting that the situation is scary and you are concerned, too, is not enough. Equally important is giving reassurance and showing how to make choices calmly, using love as the guide, not fear.

Give reassurance, facts, and ideas for positive action.

First, address their fear. In the preceding example, you might say, "No, we are not going to move." Then clarify the issue with facts appropriate for their ages. You could turn on the faucet and show that there is water, but explain that everyone will have to be careful about using too much water until there is more rain. With this approach you are being honest, giving the facts, explaining what can be done to help the situation, and giving reassurance of safety. You have also given a great example of how to handle scary news.

Remember that reassurance and clarification should be the same whether the child's fear is based on "real" scary news or on an imagined threat. If your child comes to you and says, "Joe says that all the people who drive black cars are bad guys," you still need to address the fear with honesty, with facts, and with reassurances of their safety.

Don't overload children with too much information.

Remember that information alone is not enough for preparation. Keep in mind your children's ages and stages of development when you share information that could be disturbing. The guidelines mentioned in chapter two can be helpful when deciding how much detail to share:

1. Is this information unavoidable?
2. Is this information necessary?
3. Does this information offer an opportunity for growth and deeper understanding in any way?

4. Are there signs that my child is ready for this information? (Have they asked relevant questions? Do they exhibit understanding of related concepts?)

As children grow older and can discuss issues in more depth, give them more information and include them more in decisions.

Older children would be able to help your water conservation efforts in concrete ways and may even have helpful suggestions. They will also benefit greatly from taking positive action. Working alongside family and friends to tackle a scary situation can be a positive experience they will benefit from forever.

Look to other adults for your own comfort.

When we are frightened it is natural to turn to whoever is closest for comfort. Remember that you are the parent and burdening your children with adult concerns will only add to their fears and gives them more responsibility than they are prepared to handle. Seek out adults to share your fears and thoughts with, when your children are not present.

When discussing a threat or crisis and evaluating options, teach about reliable sources of information.

Scary news of all kinds is magnified with rumors, conjecture, and misinformation. Children must learn that everything they hear may not be true and that even adults can be misinformed. Teach them with your example that information should be confirmed before making critical decisions.

Children will quickly notice that not everyone responds to threatening news the same way.

Even young school-age children can be taught to discriminate between fact and opinion and to understand priorities. Some issues, like a drought, may be a fact, but taking action to defend against that threat may be a higher priority and more stressful for a farmer than for an office worker. The best actions to take may be a matter of opinion. Pointing out that scary news will affect lives in different ways will help your children develop empathy and a greater awareness of people's diverse circumstances.

Sometimes news is scary because facts are few and responses are so diverse.

The Y2K issue is a good example of scary news on a global scale that was controversial and provoked many responses. Our family had friends who took precautions we didn't feel were necessary, such as stockpiling food and other provisions. Children may become confused when they see adults they trust making different decisions than yours. But this is a learning opportunity also and a chance for them to see you treat other opinions with respect.

With teenagers and young adults who are mature enough to watch television and are developing discrimination, talk about how television news is presented.

Help them to understand that meaningful information that is abstract or difficult to present with only a few camera shots is not given airtime. Sex and violence, tragedy and destruction make riveting pictures and have strong emotional appeal, so that is what is shown. Follow one news story on several channels and compare the coverage, then read a newspaper article about the same story and compare how much real information you obtain from each source.

Discrimination is an especially essential skill if you rely on television and radio for information. News programs compete for their share of the viewing audience, so they have become less about information and more about entertainment—leading to the descriptive term "infotainment." The Rocky Mountain Media Watch group has actually petitioned the Federal Trade Commission arguing that it is false and deceptive advertising for local programs, which entertain more than inform, to call themselves "news."

Presentations on the twenty-four-hour news channels are disjointed, repetitive—and also sensational. Multiple topics are presented with scrolling text, talking newscasters, screen-within-a-screen video, and live, remote transmissions. I was very disturbed to learn of a nine-year-old boy who was permitted to watch many hours of news every day because he "liked" it. This young child watched coverage of the terrorists attacks on New York City and Washington D.C., and then woke his mother to tell her about it. When I watch the news channel to catch up on world events, I am unable to clearly translate all the information being displayed out of context; I *know* a nine-year-old cannot do it.

Apart from the trauma of watching live tragedy every day, there is danger in the pessimistic worldview presented by the news media. Nothing is offered to balance the frightening picture of constant violence, destruction, and deceit happening around the world. Nothing tells us of life's joys that hold the world together but rather leads us to believe that we should be in a state of perpetual crisis. In a 1999 survey conducted by *CBS News*, crime was cited as the most important problem the country will face in the twenty-first century.[2] In a 2000 survey conducted by *ABC News*, 82 percent of respondents reported that their perception of the crime problem is based on what they see or read in the media and not on personal experience.[3] And according to a 2000 FBI report, since 1992 the rate of violent crime has been *decreasing*.[4] Feeding fear and killing joy may not be the intentional purpose of the media, but it certainly is a common side effect in media consumers who want to stay "informed" about world events.

In sharp contrast to this kind of news media is the monthly newsletter my nine-year-old son decided to write and share with friends and relatives. His stories are filled with the happy times we share—the birthdays, milestones, achievements, and funny events that define the world we choose to live in. I love finding out what he thinks is important news; it always makes me smile.

THE ABILITY TO discriminate and make conscious choices about when, how, and why to react defensively is essential for survival in our complex, multimedia world. Our children will be faced with many more decisions than we can imagine, and we have no way of coaching them in all the appropriate responses. But we can teach them to take responsibility for their choices, thoughtfully consider the options, and always try to make decisions based on where love leads them, rather than on where fear pushes them.

1 Hunter House Publishers, 2004
2 Public Agenda, New York, NY http://www.publicagenda.org
3 same as above
4 same as above (I checked out the stats in several places and can get another source if needed)

Chapter 7

Listen to the heart

Balance intellectual assessment with inner guidance

A woman I knew moved with her two young boys into the city from the quiet countryside. They were all accustomed to freely roaming the fields and woods near their home, so when the boys discovered a park several blocks from their new house they naturally wanted to play there. My friend allowed them to go together and play, without adult supervision. She mentioned this to me one day and asked if I would be comfortable doing the same. I told her that in light of the recent highly publicized disappearance of two girls in the area, the age of her sons, and the city environment, I thought it was too risky. I wasn't comfortable letting my children go to our neighborhood park without an adult. She told me she had been ignoring her own misgivings, but after our conversation she planned to supervise her boys more carefully.

Inner Guidance

Trusting inner guidance is the most important tool parents have for making decisions. Evaluating risks and making choices for children is hard work and a heavy responsibility that lasts a long time. But our quiet inner voice can make decision making easier. Whether you feel that inner voice as intuition, spiritual awareness, the Holy Spirit, a guardian angel, or the heart's wisdom, it is there to help.

When children open the door to a stranger while you are in the bathroom, race through the kitchen while you are holding a pot of boiling water, or jump down the stairs, three at a time, with scissors in hand, they are not *choosing* to risk disastrous consequences. Children of all ages, especially teenagers, do not have an understanding of their own physical danger or mortality; if they understood the risks as we do, they couldn't be children.

As children grow and learn to make risky decisions on their own, we hope that they also learn to use their inner guidance to help them. We need to teach by our example and give them opportunities to make their own decisions, to practice the process, and to experience listening to their inner voice.

I remember visiting my mother with my two young sons and setting off after dark on the two hour drive home. Thirty miles outside town I stopped at a rest stop, and when I tried to start the car again, the engine was dead. I called a tow truck from a pay phone and we were able to jump-start the battery. I called my husband and discussed the situation.

A sweet elderly couple stopped at the car to check on the children and me and offer advice.

I sat in the car and talked it over with my eight-year-old son; his brother was asleep. I told him that chances were good the car would be fine for the rest of the trip and we would get home to our own beds. We also wanted to get home for a commitment I had in the morning. But I did not have a cell phone, we might have to stop again, it was late and dark, and I was concerned about being stranded with two little kids to care for. I let my son help me weigh the option of turning around and going back to grandma's. We would have to unpack again, and I would miss my appointment. But

Whether you feel that inner voice as intuition, spiritual awareness, the Holy Spirit, a guardian angel, or the heart's wisdom, it is there to help.

we could have the car checked and make the trip home in the daylight. I also explained that beyond any logical reasons to turn back was the feeling I had that we should, which was not the same as being afraid to continue. We concluded that we liked the second option better, so we headed back and surprised my mom.

I certainly wasn't going to let an eight-year-old make the decision, but I included him in the process so he could see what decision making was like for an adult. I wanted him to understand that I was weighing more than the facts; I was trying to listen to the inner direction I was feeling.

Assessing Risk

One difficulty of living with one scary news story after another is that evaluating risks and making decisions becomes even more difficult. In today's media hyperbole, words like crisis, urgent, and threatening are commonplace. According to the news, daily activities such as shopping at the mall or going to school are filled with danger. So, to be able to assess risk realistically we really have to pay attention to find the facts behind the emotional headlines.

Look from diet to car seats to sun exposure, our previous risk assessments have changed because of recent scientific advancements. We once thought that washing with hot water and soap was enough to kill germs and make our laundry smell clean. Then scientists found that many microbes survived normal soap so we switched to antibacterial soap for everything from grimy hands to dirty socks. Then new studies revealed that antibacterial soap created resistant bacteria and other studies showed no advantage with such soaps, anyway. I find it hard to believe that buying soap is the complex, high-risk issue advertisers would have me believe, and I don't have time to study the latest research before going to the grocery store, so I buy what is on sale. But I actually find myself hesitating sometimes and wondering if I have made the right choice—whether I am leaving my children vulnerable to some deadly microscopic organism.

Scientific study will continue to bring us new information; some of it will help us make decisions that may improve our lives. Scary news stories will continue to worry us and perhaps change our behavior. But there is no new way for us to analyze all the options and find the best choices for our children. The tough question for us will still be: What do I *feel* is the right thing to do?

The intellect will assess the risks of an action, but the feeling in the heart tells us if the right decision has been made and whether we are moving toward the heart's joy and expansion, or toward its fear and contraction. A friend once told me that she had an internal "joy barometer" she referred to when making life choices. A falling barometer warned her that she needed to make some different choices and bring more joy into her life.

More Joy

Moving toward joy is not always the same as taking the less risky path. A friend told me of a woman who had a family vacation planned, including a tour of NASA, before the Sept. 11 terrorist attacks. After those events people all over the country changed traveling plans because of the threat advisory level that was in effect, but this woman continued with her vacation and took her family to NASA. Despite all the security checks, thorough searches of their belongings, strict rules concerning all activities, and the constant presence of armed guards, they had a wonderful time and an unforgettable experience. Staying home would have been a decision based on fear. They moved toward greater joy by going on their vacation and enjoying the experience together. Another person in the same position may have felt unsettling fear and anxiety traveling under such conditions and would have felt no joy in the opportunity.

Children need to learn that assessing the risks of any action is an important first step, but the heart and mind must work together to make the decision. This is a subtle concept, but we need to convey to them that the best decisions are based on love and not on fear. We need to teach them that asking, "What is the right thing to do?" and "Where will I experience more opening of the heart?" is the best way to touch their inner guidance. If one option appears too risky and we just turn the other way to avoid whatever worries us, we haven't *really* made a choice and we may not even see other roads that hold more promise.

But as parents we want to point our children away from what peers and the media present as cool and toward developing a strong inner barometer that will guide them.

Making decisions based on the opinions of others also leads to contraction of the heart and stifling of inner guidance. Our children live in an age that encourages extreme behavior and extreme risks. The popularity of high-risk sports and the media spotlight on those willing to risk permanent injury or death for an adrenaline rush and fleeting recognition of their peers testifies to how little value we place on inner contentment and calm reflection. The U.S. Centers for Disease Control and Prevention reports that the number of injuries from sports and recreational activities during 1997–1999 was higher than the number of injuries from car crashes during the same period![1]

Taking Risks

Advertisers for all kinds of products and services for young people are using extreme behavior for promoting their products. Even youth Bibles and related scripture study guides try to appeal to the teen market by describing scripture as being "extreme" and by giving "on the edge" answers to tough questions. The edgy graphics look like sports logos, and the editorial reviews try to hook the readers by using words and phrases like *cutting edge*, *thrill seekers*, *dare to crack open the pages*, *revolutionary*, and *are you up to the challenge*?

I don't fault the publishers and advertisers who are just trying to compete in an increasingly brutal marketplace. But as parents we want to point our children away from what peers and the media present as cool and toward developing a strong inner barometer that will guide them through all their decisions as their lives unfold.

Everyone is a risk taker to some degree, whether risks are physical, financial, career, relationship, or parenting. We need individuals in all arenas of life who have the courage to take risks and blaze new trails, contributing knowledge and experience that enriches all of society. Even those extreme sports enthusiasts may help us better understand human endurance (or prompt new discoveries in the treatment of traumatic injuries). Risking financial security to explore new career opportunities, risking social ridicule by befriending someone who is different, risking your child's anger and rejection by saying no can help us all grow personally and societally. But, it is the quiet inner voice of truth that will lead us in the right direction, regardless of the apparent outward risks and benefits of the choices at hand.

Being ignorant of the consequences and blindly going forth is not the same as courageously facing the odds and doing your best. Many have been labeled heroes in retrospect, after the excitement is over and the risks are seen clearly in hindsight, even though at the time action was taken in complete ignorance of those risks. A friend of my father's, who had many medals to show for his military service, once told us of one of the many amazing incidents that marked his career. He described with more than a little amusement how he was awarded a medal for falling into a foxhole, only to discover it was occupied by three enemy soldiers and then fighting his way out again. In countless other moments he courageously faced overwhelming risk and knowingly moved forward anyway. But he found it ironic that he was awarded a medal for the one time he blindly stepped into trouble and happened to survive to tell the tale.

As our children grow, my husband and I convey to them that many of our decisions regarding careers, finances, education, home, and family may appear illogical to others, but we make our choices based on inner guidance and faith, in addition to consideration of the facts. We want them to see beyond what is obvious and logical on the surface to a deeper level of understanding.

When teaching children how to assess risks and make choices, remember these three points:

1. Gather information and understand as much as possible about the situation before making a decision. But don't rely too much on the intellect, even if there is little information; your heart can still lead you to what is right.
2. After reviewing the facts, dig deeper and try to determine in which direction your inner guidance is pointing you. Don't stifle your inner voice; encourage it to speak out by listening carefully.
3. Make your decision based on love, not fear. Look for the opportunity to grow, expand your sympathies, and deepen your awareness.

Following those steps will ensure that the decision is right, even if it looks wrong by someone else's standards.

Suggestions

When it is appropriate, explain the reasons for some of the decisions you must make on a daily basis.

Consider your children's ages and levels of understanding and give them more information than just a yes or no answer. What led you to believe that the risk was too great, or why do you think it is acceptable? This can be tricky, because the parent's desire to teach often does not match the child's desire to learn. My children often walk away as soon as yes or no is out of my mouth, even though I am prepared to share my reasoning in much greater detail. They have even teased me about giving them long-winded answers to simple questions.

At other times my children will persist in asking what my reasons are when I feel too busy to explain. Sometimes it is an attempt to badger me into submitting, but usually it is a sign that I need to make the time to explain because they just don't understand. I have found that if I don't explain they will usually conclude that my concerns are completely about their behavior, and they walk away feeling punished.

When appropriate, let your children see you struggle with difficult choices and even let them offer advice.

Occasionally, I will be frustrated and undecided about an issue and will ask my children what they would do under the same circumstances. Sometimes their answers are predictably egocentric ("Well, I would let the kid do whatever he wanted..."), but other times they offer helpful insights. More important is the opportunity it offers them to practice valuable skills.

Whenever possible, offer opportunities for your children to make decisions on their own and experience the results of their choices.

As children grow, choices will change from which outfit to wear to more difficult choices such as choosing between two fun activities or how to spend money. Each choice is practice. Our job continues to be assessing which decisions are too risky for children to make on their own until we have to let go completely and leave it all up to them.

When other families make different choices than you do, let it be a doorway for discussion about assessing risks, making hard decisions, and respecting other's decisions.

A coworker of mine proudly related a story about her eight-year-old daughter, Corrie. Corrie had a large trampoline she loved to play on but her friend was not allowed on it because the friend's parents felt there was too much risk for injury. Corrie was upset with the decision. Rather than respecting the other parents' point of view, Corrie's mother explained that, unfortunately, some people missed out on a lot of fun because they were too afraid. She was very proud and pleased when her daughter responded with disdain, "Well, why don't they just sit on a chair and never move then?" Her mom thought Corrie was quite precocious to realize how silly some people were.

Corrie's mom missed a wonderful opportunity to discuss how all parents must assess risks and make decisions for their children. I think my children have learned valuable lessons about taking risks and making choices by observing other families and talking about why other parents make different choices for their children. They have noticed how some parents are more tolerant of physical risks, such as allowing bike riding without a helmet, but are very concerned about exposure to violence in computer games. Other parents may closely control money their children earn although they are comfortable with their children being home alone at a young age.

Discuss how TV and video games portray risky activities in an unrealistic way.

We coined a phrase in our house, "cartoon physics," that we use to describe the actions and consequences we see in movies and games that are completely against the laws of the physical universe. We often joke about it, and we also have more serious discussions about what the real risks and possible consequences would be if real people tried to do the same things.

Above all, try to show your children that inner guidance is the strongest reason for making a decision.

Try not to make decisions, even minor ones, with anxiety and restlessness. Practice taking a moment to be calm and still, pay attention to the inner pull you feel that is leading you toward greater love and truth, and learn to trust the guidance despite what the intellectual concerns are.

Help your children become aware of and use their intuition also. Talk to them about how they feel when they make a choice or decide what to do about a difficult situation. Help them to identify what made them go in the direction they did. Ask them if they had a feeling of peace or calmness. Did they feel anxious or confident? Was there inner happiness or a feeling of loss? Perhaps their feelings reminded them of another experience.

USUALLY WE HAVE THE TIME to consider our options, to calmly feel what is the best decision for ourselves, our children, our family. We all have fears about making the right decision in more dramatic circumstances, when there is no time to calmly consider all the options. If we must make some life-changing decision in a *moment*, will we know what is right? Fortunately, inner guidance can be as fast as we need it to be, but we have to practice listening. Practice when the stakes are small and you have all the time you need to listen. Help your children practice their inner awareness now, and when they need to make critical decisions we cannot foresee or prepare them for, they will naturally turn inward and listen carefully.

1 Healthday News, June 20, 2003

Chapter 8

Live in the Present

*Live in the present without debilitating worry
for the future or regret for the past.*

A senior devil's assistant, with the odd name of Screwtape,
writes letters of advice to his nephew. Screwtape knows all
the insidious ways to win a soul over to his side; his counsel
is compiled in *The Screwtape Letters* by C. S. Lewis. The
experienced Screwtape carefully explains to his naïve nephew
that their mission is easiest to accomplish in those people
who live their lives worrying about the future, the next easier
those people who dwell in the past. However, the task of
capturing a soul is almost impossible when trying to turn
someone who lives in the present:

> For the Present is the point at which time touches
> eternity . . . . . . In a word, the Future is, of all
> things, the thing *least like* eternity. It is the most
> completely temporal part of time—for the Past is

frozen and no longer flows, and the Present is all lit
up with eternal rays.

We relive the past, illogically trying to change its frozen state or torturing ourselves with regret over what we see there. We anticipate, plan for, and count on the future even though it doesn't exist. The present is the point at which time touches eternity—because spirit is timeless, with no yesterday and no tomorrow, only now.

Living in the present is a tremendous challenge; it is an attitude I believe is very difficult to maintain and easy to let go of. When my son was about six years old, he began interrupting every activity with questions about what we were going to do next. At first I patiently explained or offered options, until I realized that all our energy was used discussing future activities with very little attention given to the current task. Then I changed my tactics. When he asked about what we were going to do next, I reminded him that we were going to finish our activity before talking about the next one. It took a while, but he gradually learned to stop his questions and focus more on the present moment. It was valuable practice for me as well, but ten years and two more children later, I'm still struggling with focusing on the present.

An Attitude of the Spirit

What I am describing is an internal perspective, an attitude of the spirit; it really has little to do with external circumstances. But our intellect wants to quantify it, to shape the idea in an external way that we can see and touch. So when we are told to live in the present, our minds responds: "If I lived only for today, there would be no food on the table tomorrow." "What about my savings account, my college plan for the kids, my goals, my efforts to improve things for future generations?" "Even my prayers and my spiritual efforts are done with the hope that I can improve in the future and learn from the past." "My past has made me what I am; I can't pretend it never happened!"

The concept of living for today could be misunderstood and could lead to self-centered and destructive paths. Living for today could be interpreted as careless disregard for the consequences of harmful behavior or complete absorption in selfish desires without thought for anyone who gets in the way. It could mean burning all history books, photo albums, and other reminders of the past. A depressing extreme would be to have no children, because any parent knows that it is impossible to keep one's heart and mind completely out of the past or future when living with children.

If we reject these negative, simplistic interpretations and look more optimistically, we still have difficulty. Couldn't we say, "I *am* focused on the present—at the present, I'm very worried about my future!"

"Live each day as if it were your last." This old adage is meant to remind us of our mortality. Telling your loved ones how you feel about them and healing conflicts when you can *is* a good practice, for the opportunity may not come again. However, if we really live today as if tomorrow we will die, what would we do? When discussing this topic with a friend, she said, "If this *really* were my last day on earth, I wouldn't want to spend it at work." We can't spend each day tearfully bidding farewell to family or blowing our savings on the last big fling, only to wake in the morning and do it all over again.

"Today is the first day of the rest of your life." I grew up with this popular sentiment appearing on posters and bumper stickers. I think this is closer to what we are aiming for; it implies positive action and perseverance. But I always thought this saying carried a subtle but heavy burden for success. If today is "good" in some way, then that is supposed to bode well for my future. But what if today is "bad"? Does that mean I've marred my chances for a good future? Or perhaps I just start all over again tomorrow—in which case it feels as if I never get anywhere; I'm always back at square one.

The trouble with both of these sayings is that they point outward. What I am describing is an attitude of the spirit, a way of being, not something that must be accomplished and checked off a list.

Be in the Moment

Living in the present *means allowing the full possibility for this moment to happen, unhampered by regret or fear.* Living with an open heart, accepting the guidance and love that exists *now* allows us to experience love in all we do. We have so much to do, so much we are responsible for. Being in the present does not mean being passive; it is a dynamic state.

Even as we plan for the future, examine the past, and act in the present, we really have control only over how we choose to *be* in each moment.

It's easy to see how being fully present in joyful moments is desirable. We *want* to drink in the experience of holding a sleeping child, looking into our lover's eyes, listening to the crash of the ocean surf, or watching a sky full of stars. These are moments when we shut out fear and worry, and we naturally touch eternity. But what of the moments that are difficult, painful, frightening? And what of the mundane, everyday moments that connect our days? As a delightful greeting card of Mary Englebreit's says, "Life is just so *daily*!"

We need to stop yanking our spirit back and forth between the past and the future and make a home for it here, in the present, where we experience true joy.

The mundane, ordinary moments are when we practice for the difficult times. If we learn to feel the presence of spirit in our routines, in the small things we experience each day, then we are able to connect with eternity even in the horrible times. In *The Hiding Place*, Corrie ten Boom tells how her sister, Betsie, urged her to tell people about their experience in the Nazi concentration camps: "...must tell people what we have learned here. We must tell them that there is no pit so deep that He is not deeper still. They will listen to you, Corrie, because we have been here." Corrie had experienced the presence of spirit in every moment and realized that that presence was not dependent on outward circumstance.

No matter the outward circumstances, spirit and eternity exist completely and wholly in the here and now; it is only our perception that separates us from the "eternal rays." Living in the present means accepting and even embracing this moment, for there is no other. We need to stop yanking our spirit back and forth between the past and the future and make a home for it *here*, in the present, where we experience true joy.

Think about coaching a child to shoot a basketball or drive a car: the most common advice is, "relax and concentrate." To do something well, relaxation is required to allow energy to flow unimpeded by physical or mental tension. We must also concentrate fully on the task at hand, pushing aside thoughts of what *has* happened (the past) or what *might* happen (the future). To live in the present, relaxation and concentration is also the best advice.

Concentration

The definition of concentration is to focus attention one pointedly. Our minds are so often like busy bumblebees, zooming from one thing to the next, hardly pausing before moving on to the next tempting thought. Upon deeper consideration, however, the bee comparison doesn't work. The bumblebee is fulfilling its purpose and accomplishing the task it was born to do. And I would hazard an unscientific guess that the bumblebee is concentrating completely on the task at hand, without distracting musings about tomorrow or yesterday. Our lack of concentration prevents us from accomplishing the great things we were born to do. Our tomorrows and yesterdays crowd into today until there is no room for joy *right now*.

Concentration with tension is ineffective and wasteful. Tension in mind and body steals energy away from what we are trying to do and serves only to make tasks more difficult. When we observe people who are skilled at what they do, whether actor, singer, or mechanic, what is most apparent is the how effortless their tasks appear. Why? They are relaxed and are not tense. Regret for the past and worry for the future cause tension, which makes the job of living in the present much harder than it has to be.

The scary news we experience daily challenges our ability to connect with the joy in the present. Focusing on and feeling the joy that lives in the *now* must have been a bit easier before technology became commonplace. The stories of Laura Ingalls Wilder and her life as an American pioneer are favorites in our house. Her books, such as *Little House on the Prairie,* describe the ordinary details of her family's life as well as the extraordinary joys and sorrows. Survival was a constant struggle yet Wilder describes such joy in what each day offered. She showed amazing acceptance and wholehearted participation in every experience. Perhaps her perceptions were unusual. But if she had been able to see all the scary news of her time, in the vivid detail we have today, her life would have been a lot harder.

I was enjoying lunch out with my daughter one afternoon when I picked up a newspaper left by a previous patron. A glance at the headline, "Three year old Seriously Injured in Fall From a Third Story Window," pulled my attention away from her and into shock and morbid curiosity as I read the story. My daughter continued to chat and enjoy her lunch, but my attention was only partly with her as I read the details of the accident that had nothing to do with my present moment and served only to shift my spirit into another time and place. I tried to shake off my emotions after reading the story and give my attention back

Don't give up—it is not impossible for your children to learn how to concentrate.

to my daughter, but some of the joy I could have experienced there at the sunny lunch table was lost because I forgot to keep my awareness with my daughter and our time together.

It takes extra effort to fully experience what is trying to happen right now when we have constant reminders of scary events—past, present, and future—all around us. It's not a terrible thing to read the paper during lunch, but so many things pull us out of *now* that days and years can go by without our ever experiencing what today offers. Focusing on the present requires tremendous will power, patience, and concentration. An invaluable gift to our children is helping them learn concentration in all things so they have the ability to focus on today and what they are doing at this moment, which will bring more joy into their lives than any other skill they can cultivate.

Concentration is a difficult skill to teach directly. The best thing parents can do is to reduce stimulation in your children's environment and then provide plenty of opportunity to practice concentration in a variety of settings. Don't give up—it is not impossible for your children to learn how to concentrate.

Parents often become more concerned about what has to be done and forget to note how things are going right now. If your children are playing contentedly and are quietly focused, give them more time and don't interrupt to get teeth brushed or toys picked up. Protect them from interfering siblings and friends because this is valuable and essential practice. Later, point out how concentrated and focused they were and talk about how that experience felt. Ask what helped their concentration and what distracted them. Provide what they need to encourage concentration during other activities.

Suggestions for Helping Children Put Aside Worry about the Past

I once heard memory described as a gift given to enable us to recall all the good that comes into our lives. Using memory to recall past hurts and wrongs is an abuse of this precious gift. Living in the past and wishing for the power to do it over differently are common debilitating habits that can allow feelings of helplessness, failure, shame, and anger to become like open wounds that cause chronic pain. We can help our children establish good habits early and avoid living with those kinds of wounds.

Help your children find "closure" to painful and upsetting experiences and move on emotionally.

Establish a habit of praying together every night and giving the day's experiences to God.

Lead your children through the simple visualization of taking all the day's experiences and feelings and piling them up for God to take care of. They could mentally wrap their feelings like packages and stack them up.

Children can pray for anyone who may have hurt their feelings or upset them in some way.

Without laying blame or going over old arguments again, just pray for that person to feel peace and to let go of bad feelings, also.

If your children want to go over an event and have regrets about how they behaved, help them think about what could be done differently next time.

Give them an opportunity to talk about what helped or what didn't help the situation, even role play if they really want to work it out. Just saying the words they wish they had said can establish a positive direction for the future.

If they express a desire to make amends, help them find a way to do it as soon as possible.

Writing a note, drawing a picture, giving flowers, making cookies, doing a chore, or being a surprise helper are all ways they can apologize and express their feelings.

One of my sons was very little when we planted new trees in our front yard. He was angry because they were in the area he was used to playing in, so he said he didn't like the trees and hoped they would die. After a while, it was clear that one tree was not doing very well and we were concerned it wouldn't survive. Our son was stricken with remorse and was sure his angry words were the reason the tree wasn't growing. I reassured him that it wasn't his fault, but it became clear that he didn't believe me and if the tree died he would blame himself. He helped to water the tree, but he wanted to do more. So with my help he wrote a note of apology. He told the tree he was sorry and that he really wanted it to live and grow strong and tall. Then we buried the note at the tree's roots. The tree didn't die, and my son tells me he now feels like the tree is his friend.

Teach a simple affirmation to learn acceptance for each day's events. "I accept today as a gift, with joy and blessings inside."

Each individual experiences grief and loss differently.

Children can have feelings of grief over a minor event like losing a favorite toy, but when a major event is life changing or if your child is having difficulty moving out of grief into a normal routine, professional help can be invaluable.

Suggestions for Helping Children Put Aside Worry about the Future

Worrying about tomorrow tends to be an adult trait, because we feel the responsibility for making things happen. But kids will live in tomorrow by anxiously anticipating a fun thing, like a birthday or allowance, or dreading a difficult thing, like a test, or vaccination shots. We wouldn't want to turn off their eager anticipation or surprise them with difficulties and no preparation, but we can gently remind them to keep their hearts in the present.

Use a calendar to help young children plan for events.

Even nonreaders can count days on a calendar and mark off days until a big event. They can use stickers to note birthdays or holidays. My daughter seems to have less anxiety about an event if she knows how many days away it is and can count it out on the calendar.

Reassure them that they have the skills to successfully cope with anticipated events.

Acknowledge your children's feelings of anxiety about an upcoming challenge and reassure them they have the skills to cope successfully. If needed, help them to gain necessary skills and become prepared.

Make up fun and unique special days.

"Wear pink day" or "Make Daddy a surprise lunch day" or "Take teddy bear for a walk day" is a fun way to teach that every day is a special gift.

Teach your children to savor the present.

Try pausing during an activity and ask everyone to share one thing about "right now". Examples: "Right now I can feel the breeze from the fan on my face." "Right now I can hear the whistle of a train going by." "Right now I can see three things that are my favorite color." "Right now I'm feeling happy and relaxed."

Make a game of noticing three special things about each day. Include it as part of your daily activities, the discussion at mealtime, or a bedtime ritual.

IF OUR CHILDREN are able to experience joy and love in the present, scary news will not have the power to shake their world the way it can in those who allow their spirit to live in the future or the past. Feeling the firm foundation of now will enable them to make decisions calmly, without fear. If we can help our children understand that joy exists, unchanging, in this moment, then perhaps they will remember to look for it even when circumstances appear dreadful

Beauty, Goodness, and Joy

See and appreciate the goodness and beauty that exists around us.

Keeping a positive attitude when circumstances are difficult is good practice. Actually *recognizing* and *experiencing* goodness and beauty every day, however, goes beyond optimism to a deep personal awareness of the truth that goodness and beauty exist everywhere. Noticing the beauty that exists around us is really an extension of the idea presented in chapter 8: living fully in the present. For if we are anxious about the future or are regretting the past, we will miss the present moment that is offering us beauty and joy. We have to shift our consciousness and bring beauty into focus, like a skilled photographer who can make the subject appear clear and sharp against a fuzzy background.

Beauty is Everywhere

One evening my daughter and I were playing ball in front of our house. During a pause in our play I noticed that the sky was changing color, and I looked up at the clouds. We can't see much of the western horizon from our house, but that evening the sunset seemed to be happening directly overhead. Somehow I felt connected with the crimson sky as the colors and clouds shifted and played away the end of the day. Although it lasted only a few minutes, the experience changed my consciousness. I watch the sky all the time now, and I am often thrilled with what I see there.

∞

These may also be realities, but where do you want your spirit to live: among the pain and suffering or among the clouds?

∞

For me, those few moments did more to affirm the reality of goodness and beauty in the universe than any philosophical argument could. Some would say that the lovely colors were a result of pollution in the atmosphere, or would remind me that while I looked at the sky people suffered and children cried. These may also be realities, but where do you want your spirit to live: among the pain and suffering or among the clouds?

Being aware of beauty and goodness is neither a denial of harsher realities nor a refusal to accept or act to change the ugly side of life. It is a confirmation that beauty and good-ness also exist as a part of our reality. When we live in that broader reality, we are able to see *solutions* to pain and suffering; we can feel fear shrink as joy grows. Joy is our true nature. Joy opens the heart to possibilities we don't see when we look with eyes full of fear.

Just as we feed our children healthy foods and vitamins, we must fill them with positive thoughts and experiences to keep their spirits healthy and strong. We must be aware of the negative messages our children encounter every day and fight back with positive messages of beauty and goodness.

In chapter seven, I mentioned public opinion polls con-ducted in 1999 and 2000 regarding people's perception of crime in America. Although violent crime has decreased since 1992, polls showed that it is perceived as the biggest problem we face in the new millennium and that those perceptions are shaped by what people saw portrayed in the media, not by their personal experience's. In light of recent world events the answer to the questions asked may now be different, but most important is that *media influence and the resulting fear can be so strong as to override factual information and our actual experience of the world.*

Make Room for Goodness and Beauty

Have you ever taken a walk with a young child and found yourself stopping to look at every bug, flower, rock, and leaf along the way? Young children are naturally curious and are learning about their environment through exploration. Each detail they encounter they experience with wonder, and each experience confirms for them the reality of beauty in the world. Young children *expect* wonderful things around every corner.

But sadly, as most children grow up, that wonder and expectation of beauty is gradually lost, often not because of experience, but because of the messages received from the world. The negative messages and frightening images children are exposed to can fill a child's consciousness and leave little room for anything else. Expectation of delight is replaced with expectation of fear and ugliness. I remember telling my daughter that I didn't want her to watch something on television I thought would be scary for her. This four-year-old very casually responded, "It's okay, Mom, I'm used to ugly stuff now."

Our local library is a short walk from our house and the whole family is grateful because we all love to read. I am pleased to see that there continues to be a steady supply of new children's books despite the mass appeal of television and electronic entertainment. But I can't help but notice how many of the popular children's books have nothing beautiful, hopeful, or inspiring to offer. On more than one occasion I've been disturbed to see books on display in the children's area that feature nightmarish cover art and gruesome titles. The librarians are always puzzled by my concern when I point out that such displays are not appropriate.

I'm not advocating censorship or holding every book to a Pollyanna-type standard. But I think one of our jobs as parents is to make sure there is always room for goodness and beauty in our children's lives. We must because the world will *not*. The world will give them what was so graphically described on the cover of a mail-order book catalog: "COOL, WEIRD, FUNNY, GROSS—Books for the kind of kid you are!" Another catalog recommends teen reading lists that are heavy with "real life" stories of drug addiction, alcoholism, kidnapping, abuse, home-lessness, and other fear-laden topics such as suicide, racism, and apocalyptic events. If the news headlines aren't scary enough, our children can read about these horrors in their leisure time, too!

One of our jobs as parents is to make sure there is always room for goodness and beauty in our children's lives.

I overheard my teenage son try to explain to his stubborn younger brother why the books by James Herriot (an English country veterinarian) were worth reading. "These stories are just *nice*, they make you feel good. It would be good for you to read a *nice* story," reassuring me that he still has an appreciation for simple goodness and beauty.

Train Your Consciousness

The beauty I refer to has nothing to do with the politically correct standards of physical beauty, fashion, or design. It has nothing to do with affluence or good taste; the media, Hollywood, or popular fads do not determine it. True beauty and goodness touch the soul and open the heart. They resonate with our true nature, reminding us who and what we really are—children of spirit and light with souls of eternal joy. Beauty can be a warm smile from a stranger, the familiar touch of a loved one, the quiet moment before sunrise, the sound of the ocean or uplifting music, a picture your child drew, the smell of fresh bread, the softness of a baby's skin, a drink of cold water on a hot day, the sparkle of snow, or a million other wondrous and glorious blessings that life offers each of us with astounding frequency.

When a child's heart and mind is full of goodness and beauty, there isn't room for fear and darkness.

Training ourselves to bring beauty and goodness into focus is not difficult; it's a matter of adjusting our hearts and minds. If you *want* to see beauty and goodness, train your consciousness always to be on the lookout. With each experience, your heart will open a bit more and your awareness will increase.

I have a friend who is a motorcycle enthusiast and for him a motorcycle is a thing of beauty. He was eating at a restaurant with his family one day and noticed what looked like a rare motorcycle in the parking lot of the hotel next door. Only a small part of the machine was visible from his vantage point, so after his meal he went to check and it was, as he had suspected, a beautiful and uncommon kind of bike. This was a thrill, but even bigger thrill was finding out that a large group of bikers was meeting at the hotel and *all* owned the same model of motorcycle! He looked around the parking lot to find his dream bike multiplied many times over. Whereas I rarely notice motorcycles, my friend notices bikes and fellow bike lovers wherever he goes because his consciousness is focused on them.

After buying a new car, you may find that suddenly you are noticing the same model around every corner. When my children get new shoes, they notice other children with the same shoes. Pregnant women see other pregnant women wherever they go. This is not just an imagined experience; it happens because our consciousness changes. We suddenly have an increased awareness of something because it has become part of our experience; now we notice the same in our environment more readily.

You may know people who have trained their spirit to always live in awareness of beauty and goodness. Although based on the same principle of my friend and his motorcycles, this ability reaches far deeper and broader to encompass what Cecil Alexander describes in her poem, *Maker of Heaven and Earth*, as "all things bright and beautiful."

Those who are able to see the world in this way inspire those of us who are still working toward that goal.

I had the joy of knowing Paula, a woman who inspired everyone with her ability to appreciate and create beauty at every opportunity. She faced life's hardships without flinching, but never failed to notice the smallest detail that was pleasing or harmonious to the spirit. People like Paula joyfully recognize beauty in all forms. They notice beauty in their environment and they see goodness in the people they meet; what's more, they have the ability to share beauty with others, so just being in their presence is an experience in joy.

If you have such people in your life, make sure your children spend time with them. The lessons to be learned from them are too valuable to pass up. But if you don't know such people, it may seem impossible to see the world as joyful. We see so many difficult and disturbing things every day; how can we *really* teach our children to see beyond them?

When a child's heart and mind is full of goodness and beauty, there isn't room for fear and darkness. Almost one hundred years ago in her book, *The Secret Garden*, Frances Hodgson Burnett described how the beauty of a garden coming alive changed the lives of three people. She so eloquently explained that what the characters called "magic" was just a simple truth:

> Two things cannot be in one place.
> Where you tend a rose, my lad,
> A thistle cannot grow.

Suggestions

Provide opportunities for your children to experience beauty.

Experiencing beauty does not have to be grand and glorious. My son loves to eat by candlelight; he thinks it is wonderful and mysterious and fun. Simply lighting candles fills him with special thoughts. He is so grateful and happy that the last time we lit candles I made a silent promise to do it more often. I want him to have more lovely moments in his heart.

I love taking walks with my children. Usually it's just around the block in our city neighborhood, but we always see something we can enjoy and smile about. It may be a neighborhood cat, a new flower, or a spider's web. We have fun watching people mow their lawns or paint their houses. We may chat with someone we haven't seen for a while or watch someone learning to ride a bike, or find out there is a new baby on the block. I love going out with only the purpose of spending time together and then sharing a lovely memory.

Even more important, listen to your children and share their moments of beauty and joy.

Children usually are eager to share their view of the world and simply want you to see the wonderful things they see. Sometimes my son will stop in the frenzy of his activities and tell me something he really loves about the way the sky looks, or how the breeze feels on his face, or the way the house feels so cozy when it's stormy outside. I don't always listen like I should, but when I stop what I am doing and really *listen* to what he is trying to convey, I also feel the beauty he is experiencing in the moment. I'm so grateful that he shared it with me and that I took the time to experience it, too.

I am not much of a gardener, and I confess that most plants die under my care. But my daughter has inspired me to keep trying because she shares with me her joyful appreciation of every flower. For her every blossom is a miracle, whether it is a dandelion or an orchid. She is so happy there are flowers in the world and that there are so many varieties to amaze her; her joy has taught me to see flowers as more than a sign of gardening success or failure.

Keep ugliness in your children's environment to a minimum.

Make conscious choices for reading material, toys, games, and pictures, using your personal comfort level as a guide. You don't have to go far down the toy aisle to see toys that are horrifying and ugly or simply bizarre and unsettling. Before allowing these things in your home, think of the number of hours your children will be playing with and looking at them. You will see them, too; do you really *want* to look at them regularly? If not, then don't let it happen. The same is true of video games, posters on the walls of children's rooms, and even the clothes your children wear.

I believe one reason so many parents give their children their own bedrooms equipped with televisions and computers goes deeper than issues of privacy, autonomy, and noise control. I think they don't want to look at the ugly stuff marketed to children these days. It seems easier to try and confine all that ugliness in the back bedroom than to deal with saying no. A child's room will be different than an adult's room, but it still can be a room of peace and beauty.

Fill your heart with a collection of beauty and goodness.

Many people collect *things* because they enjoy the excitement of acquisition and ownership. The excitement is short lived, however, and they are soon hunting for the next thing to add to the collection. Why not be a collector of beautiful experiences? Teach your children that they can acquire a wonderful collection of experiences and keep them in their hearts by seeking out beauty and goodness wherever they are. Share them and relive them whenever you get a chance. At the dinner table encourage family members to share good experiences from their day. Write them down and share them in letters and journals. Find any way you can to deeply plant the reality of beauty and goodness into your child's consciousness so it cannot be uprooted in times of fear or uncertainty.

Express gratitude for the people and events in your life, and share your gratitude with your children.

Help them find ways to express their feelings of gratitude and to share them with friends and family. Some people like keeping a gratitude journal so they can reread it during difficult times. Young children could put marbles in a jar for each thing they are grateful for. Writing thank-you notes to family and friends is a good habit to establish early, so children learn to express their gratitude. Don't do it only for birthday presents. Write notes of gratitude for any blessing special friends bring into their lives.

One of my sons always groans about writing thank-you notes, and I always have to push him into it. He views it as a chore and won't be convinced that it is fun. But when he sits down and gets into the flow of expressing his gratitude, he writes beautiful notes of appreciation. His grandparents and friends always want to thank him for his lovely letters because his sincerity is felt in every line.

Share examples of people who have trained their spirit to live in beauty and goodness.

Many admirers of Mother Teresa of Calcutta are able to list all the hardships she faced and the sacrifices she made for her work. Books about her life go into great detail about the horrible conditions she worked in and the shocking suffering of the poor she served. But many who watched her missed one of the valuable lessons she taught the world. She was certainly aware of the suffering and sorrow around her, but that was not *all* she saw; that was not the focus for her.

Mother Teresa once explained that she and the nuns who worked with her did not see hopelessness, but saw the beauty and light of Christ in each soul, and their work was to serve Him joyfully. That was their focus; that is what filled their hearts and their thoughts each day.

Deliberately choose to put things in your environment that will remind you of your goal.

We can change our home environment, but have little control elsewhere. Keeping beauty and goodness in focus while dealing with the world can be very difficult. We all need reminders to keep refocusing the lens of our consciousness; suggestions in chapter 4 discuss creating a peaceful and beautiful environment in your home. Use whatever works for you and your children. I keep a picture of my friend Paula near my desk because her beautiful spirit inspires me so.

I've known people to put little pictures or quotes on the dashboards of their cars to help them during their commute. Children often spend most of their day away from home; what could you do to help remind them of beauty and goodness while you are apart? Perhaps notes in their backpacks, or lunch bags, pictures to hang in their school lockers, or special tapes to listen to while they walk to school would help them stay focused on what is right in the world.

This is a true story of such a reminder. I was driving alone through the city, with my mind wandering, when a car sped up the left lane and quickly cut in front of me. I slowed to accommodate it as my mind registered that it was a very *expensive* red sports car with a custom license plate that said GREED. I chuckled and thought, "At least he's honest!" Then my next thought was, "What a negative affirmation!" I imagined owning that car. I pictured myself seeing GREED every time I opened the garage, every time I looked for the car in a parking lot, every time I walked to the car with a friend or lifted groceries out of the trunk. I actually felt loaded down with the burden of greed. These thoughts went quickly through my mind as the car took an opening in the traffic and sped out of sight.

Just a few moments later another car sped up the left lane and cut in front of me. I noticed it was not a flashy sports car this time; it was a midsize, midprice, forgettable kind of car. But what immediately caught my eye was the custom license plate that said, BLISS. I laughed out loud at the unexpected message and felt a thrill of joy at the truth of it. As soon as I read BLISS, the car also inexplicably found an opening in the heavy traffic and was gone.

Bliss, or inexpressible joy, is the nature of the universe. How wonderful to be reminded of bliss every time you drive to work or pick up the kids. To see BLISS as you run through the parking lot in the rain or while you unlock the trunk to toss in your purchases at the mall would help contribute to your positive view of the world.

When events are frightening and hard to understand, remind your children of anything that is right or good that they can see.

This doesn't mean making light of tragedy or making up a silver lining in a bad situation. But if you look for it, there is usually an act of kindness, bravery, or hope even in awful circumstances. Since the events of Sept. 11th there has been a lot of focus on the men and women who work as police and fire fighters, and rightly so. It's natural to see the contrast between their selfless acts and the calculated cruelty of the terrorists. It is so important for children to be shown any light shining in the darkness.

> Whatever is true, whatever is honorable, whatever is
>   right,
> whatever is pure, whatever is lovely, whatever is of
>   good repute,
> if there is any excellence and if anything worthy of
>   praise,
> let your mind dwell on these things. Philippians 4:8

If you are not in the habit of noticing goodness and beauty around you or of sharing those experiences with your children, at first it may seem a bit artificial to do so. But it takes practice to banish old habits and establish new ones. The more you invite light and beauty into your life, the more you will see the value in this suggestion.

PERHAPS MOTHER THERESA could see beauty even in the most awful situations, but most of us don't have that level of understanding. There will be simply horrible situations and circumstances and it may not be possible to find any goodness connected to them. During those times, knowing that beauty and joy are real will be a source of strength that will help you survive and move on. Helping your children see and experience what is right and lovely in the world will bring them more joy now *and* give them strength and courage to draw on later.

Chapter 10

A Loving Heart

Act with love for others when faced with fear or helplessness.

All loving parents hope that when things become difficult their children will be able to act with love and compassion. We hope they will be the source of loving action and able to make a difference in the lives of others.

Reaching out to others with self-forgetfulness is possible only if there is a connection with a purpose larger than our own needs and desires. But there is something more: There must be an understanding of the nature of love.

> Make us each a channel of Thy peace.
> When in darkness, guide us from above,
> Where there is sorrow, may we sow Thy joy.
> Where there is hatred, may we share Thy love.[1]

An Infinite Source

One night as my daughter was climbing into bed she turned to me and reported that the teacher at church said if people are mean to us we are supposed to love them. She looked at me with amazement and waited for my reaction.

I said, "That seems like it would be pretty hard, doesn't it?" She slowly answered, "Yeeaahh," accompanied by a look that said "Not just hard, but impossible!"

I sat down with her and explained that we couldn't possibly love someone who hurt us with our *own* love. If it were just up to us, that really would be impossible. But we can try to love with *God's* love. Because all love comes from God, and God loves all of us even when we do wrong, we can ask God to love people through us. I told her that it still might be hard, but God would help us give His love to everyone if we are willing to try.

She went to bed visibly relieved that the burden wasn't as big as she had imagined it to be. She didn't have to make enough love for everyone; she just had to tap into the source of all love.

> *Love is not an emotion that begins in us and ends in the positive response of another. Love is a divine energy that begins in God and has no end.*
>
> Eric Butterworth[2]

From the time our children are very young we should be teaching them that real love is not something we manufacture.

Loving everyone equally, even those we don't know or those who would do us harm and never love us in return, is an impossible, overwhelming, and incredibly discouraging idea. We don't have the ability to *produce* love and pass it out in equal portions to everyone we see.

But if we think about acting as channels for the *infinite* source of love, then loving everyone becomes a possibility. When children grasp this idea, they learn to notice if love is flowing through them or if the flow of love is blocked by worry, self-doubt, fear, or other emotions that close the heart.

Giving a Memory of Love

In chapter two, I mentioned that the brain stores memories that have emotional significance differently from memories without emotions attached. Those memories are also retrieved differently; we can relive those moments with vivid clarity, experiencing them over and over. With time, the strong feelings involved usually become more of an echo of those we actually experienced and we can gain some detach-ment, but the memory and the associated emotion are forever linked in our brains and hearts.

I once attended a professional workshop about grief coun-seling. What I learned there agreed with everything I learned years later about brain physiology. Most important was when working with people who are in acute grief we must understand that it's *beyond our power to take the grief away*. This is the cause of the common feeling of helplessness we experience with deeply emotional and difficult circumstances.

We want to undo the *cause* of the grief, but that's not possible. What we *can* do is plant a memory of love and kindness. Our kindness and love gives those who are grieving a memory of sweetness, compassion, and gentleness during their time of trauma and the two memories will be stored together in the brain. Every time they retrieve the painful memory, the memory of our loving act will also be retrieved because the two will be always be entwined. The darkness of fear, pain, and loss will always have the light of love and kindness as a companion.

I spent several days in Washington, D.C., to attend my father's funeral at Arlington National Cemetery. Those days were difficult and unforgettable. An old friend of my father's took the time to tell stories of experiences they had shared facing the challenges of war, marriage to their young sweethearts, and family life. My siblings and I watched as he and my mother laughed and reminisced, and we were given a view into my father's heart we hadn't ever seen. My memories of those days of grief are always warm with the pleasure of those hours of love and kindness.

Acting with love also gives *the giver* the memory of loving instead of the feeling of helplessness. It is a way for all involved to move away from darkness and fear into light and love.

My family was shocked and saddened when a young neighbor friend died suddenly. The neighborhood was also greatly concerned for another young girl on the block who was battling cancer. The nation was recovering from the September 11 terrorist attacks that occurred a few months prior, and I could feel the grief and fears of our entire neigh-borhood pulling at my heart.

I felt compelled to do something, and my husband and I researched the possibility of finding a variety of rose that shared the name of the young girl we missed so much. We were pleased to find that such a rose did exist, only to discover that it was available only in Canada and could not be shipped to the United States. After brief consideration, we decided that a trip to Canada shouldn't stop us. Many neighbors supported our efforts. Our family shared a fun and informative trip to Canada that didn't seem like much effort at all, and we bought the special rose bushes. We then gave the girl's family the potted roses and a letter from all who had contributed.

Every time my children think of the loss of their friend, they remember the trip to Canada and the special roses we lovingly brought back. I am so grateful for those memories and the change we all felt when we took positive action.

Acting with love during times of chaos, confusion, and pain takes a great deal of energy. You may feel as if you are going against a strong current of anger, despair, and hope-lessness. But every time you take action and fight the current, you create a stronger flow of energy toward expansion and your sense of self grows beyond the boundaries you imagined you had. You act as a channel for light in the world, and your children learn how it is possible to conquer fear.

Choosing the Right Action

How we act with love—with an attitude of openness and service—is more important than *what* we do. We must follow our inspiration and find the way to be instruments that lead us toward expansion. Running for office and serving in a political way may be the perfect way for some to open their hearts, learn acceptance and humility, and feel connected to something bigger. For another, politics may only lead to frustration while cooking for others offers great joy.

Children also have different needs, desires, and personalities that will find expression in different ways. One may love being physical by cleaning up litter or planting trees, another may find joy writing letters of sympathy or encouragement, and another will take on the challenge of collecting pledges for a fundraising drive.

Ask: Where does love lead me? What brings more love into my life? Your answers will guide you.

Choosing a family project and doing it together can be fun and rewarding. Then you also share the energy and the good memories. Sometimes, though, your child may have an inspiration that the rest of the family doesn't share. If one child wants to write a letter to earthquake victims because she learned about earthquakes in school and the other children aren't interested, support her efforts and don't make everyone take part.

Follow your heart when deciding how to act with love for others and teach your children these three guidelines:

1. Act from love, not from guilt or obligation. We are bombarded with opportunities to give our time, money, signature, and groceries to help others. In response, some people give more than they really want to and then alternate between feeling guilty and feeling resentful because they allow social pressures and political correctness to dictate their choices. Others shut down their hearts and stop doing anything for anyone because it can be overwhelming to sort through all the requests for help in any logical way.

   What we want to show our children is how to open their hearts and act with love when they feel fear and sadness pulling them down. That's the time to respond with energy and action, which will draw us up and out of that downward flow. Ask: Where does love lead me? What brings more love into my life? Your answers will guide you.

2. Be careful about being attached to the results of your actions. Don't teach your children to do something only to fix a problem or "make a difference." They may never see the results of their actions, or notice any difference in outward circumstances, and they may not be able to fix the problem. Instead, teach them to act with love because it brings joy, it will change their lives, it puts them in tune with divine will, and it may help others rise out of the darkness of fear.

3. Resist the temptation to measure your efforts against someone else's actions or expectations. We want to promote in our children the habit of responding positively, and small gestures are good practice for the day when a big effort is needed. And how do we know that a small gesture won't have huge impact? If others are able to write large checks, or open their homes to the needy, or devote themselves to volunteer work full time, don't let that keep you or your children from making any gesture you feel inspired to make with love.

It is not how much we do, but how much love we put in the doing. It is not how much we give, but how much love we put in the giving.

Mother Teresa of Calcutta

Money

Money seems to be in a different category from taking action in other ways. And yet, it really isn't different. Money is energy in disguise, and acting with love in the face of fear can include using the power of money.

It is possible to give money with love and joy without feeling attached to an outcome or comparing your gift to others. It can be meaningful and worthwhile to respond to a crisis by giving money to victims or to those who provide valuable and essential services. You can share wonderful lessons when you involve your children in decisions about giving money and teaching them how to do so with love.

Money is energy in disguise, and acting with love in the face of fear can include using the power of money.

When children are very young and don't have an understanding of what money is worth, they believe any amount of money is valuable, even more so if it is shiny. They will give a sparkling penny to a friend with great drama and excitement, and their eyes will dance with the generosity they feel. Don't spoil their moment by giving a lesson on how little a penny is worth; acknowledge their gesture as kind and generous.

My five-year-old daughter held up a nickel and told me she wanted to give it to the workers who were putting windows in our house. They were nice and friendly, but I was afraid her feelings would be hurt if they laughed at her offer. So I told her it was nice to want to give them something; how about offering a piece of candy from the bowl we had on the table? She was happy with that option and her loving impulse wasn't squelched.

When your children are old enough to understand, discuss with them your decision to support a charity or donate money to help someone, whether it is a regular part of your budget or special circumstances that have inspired you. I remember feeling particularly exasperated one evening after answering the door and politely turning down yet another request for money. Traffic to my door had been unusually heavy that week, and I was suddenly aware that my children saw me say no a lot. I was concerned they may not understand my actions so I sat down with them and explained that their father and I contribute regularly to things we felt inspired to support and our decisions about giving money were made together with deep consideration. The kids said they already understood that, but I made a mental note to make sure they saw us saying yes as well as no.

Whenever possible, make your contribution of money real and meaningful for your children by taking more action than simply mailing the check. Take the amount you want to give and go shopping together for useful items, then deliver or mail them together. Research the organization you will be supporting and read about it with your children; visit the organization's office in your city or talk to a representative. If you are sending money for emergency services or relief in a city or country far away, learn about the people and culture of that area together and find out what their needs are.

Help your children express why they chose to send the money and let them write letters to send with your check. This may also get them a thank you letter in response, but don't do it for that reason.

Suggestions for things children can do:

Send letters or pictures to someone who has suffered a loss or is facing a challenge.

My son always had an interest in aircraft carriers and when we learned that the *Enterprise* was being sent back to sea and the crew wouldn't have shore leave for months, we wrote letters to the service personnel on board. We were happy thinking they might pass around our letters and pictures while far away on the ocean.

Contribute to a work that touches your children's heart or is important to someone who could use support.

Like most children, mine love animals and thought it was really fun to "adopt" wild tigers and whales by contributing to a wildlife research organization. We learned about the lives of those animals and felt connected to the natural world.

Participate in a fund raising effort that has meaning for your children.

A young friend of ours was coping with cancer and her school track team put together a fund-raising run for her. It was a huge effort, with hundreds of people involved. We watched all the runners with fascination. Some were experts with expensive athletic gear, obviously at home on the track; some were neighbors with strollers, chatting with friends as they strolled their laps; others were loyal classmates putting out a lot of energy and enjoying the team spirit.

My husband spotted a runner who stood out from the rest, and he was so moved by the teenager's dedication he went down to the track to speak to him and make a pledge in his name. The teenager was not a close friend of the girl's; he just really wanted to help. His poor clothes and shoes were not made for running miles, but he was determined to do as many laps as possible in the hot sun. When my husband discovered the small amount in pledges the teenager would collect for all his effort, he promised a larger contribution that brought a shocked smile to the boy's sweaty face. We were deeply grateful for the opportunity to witness the boy's selfless dedication and for the example of loving generosity my children saw in their father that day.

When your children donate part of their allowance or work to earn money they wish to give, their actions will have more meaning.

Your children could give up a treat and use the money they would have spent to support the cause that inspires them. For example: Give up going to the usual Saturday movie and contribute the ticket money. Older children could set a monetary goal and work until they achieve it. Younger children will be happy giving whatever they can.

- **Make care packages for a family who has lost possessions in a natural disaster or a fire.**
- **Volunteer as a family for a service organization that is responding to an emergency need.**
- **Pick up litter around your block as an act of kindness toward your neighbors.**
- **Take cookies to the local fire or police department to express your appreciation.**

- Help someone who has suffered a loss by taking care of the lawn or garden, or cleaning the house.
- Establish a habit of praying for others.

> *More things are wrought by prayer*
> *Than this world dreams of.*
>
> Alfred, Lord Tennyson, "Idylls of the King"

Prayer was discussed in chapter five as a way to comfort our children. Pray is also a loving act we can perform for others in times of need. When we pray for others we ask that God use us to bring more light and love into the world. We become channels for an infinite source of power, and the blessings multiply for those who are prayed for and those who pray. With practice, the idea of taking action by praying for others will become a simple, natural part of everyday experience; instead of an automatic contraction of the heart in response to scary news, we will have an opening of the heart and a flow of energy outward to others.

The act of dynamic, loving prayer is limited only by our inner willingness and carries the greatest power to change and heal.

When teaching children to pray for others, the form is not as important as the attitude of the heart during prayer. Outward details, such as folding hands, kneeling, closing eyes, bowing the head, lighting candles, are meant to help open the heart and put the one who prays into the right frame of mind. The outward form will be shaped by personal history and tradition, culture and religion, inspiration and convenience; but the inner offering of heart and will is what opens the floodgates and allows grace to flow in. The act of dynamic, loving prayer is limited only by our inner willingness and carries the greatest power to change and heal.

> *He prayeth well, who loveth well*
> Samuel Taylor Coleridge,
> "The Rime of the Ancient Mariner"

The right attitude for prayer can be compared to the postage placed on a letter; it gets the message carried farther than the mailbox. It will help to keep the guidelines in mind: Act from love, not from guilt or obligation; try not to be attached to the results of your prayers; don't compare how, when, or why you pray with the prayers of others.

Any loving thought can become a prayer without a lot of ceremony. It can be a quick little thought that is held and released in a moment, sent on its way like an arrow of light to spread its message of love. Everyone has little thoughts that can become arrows of light, such as, "I love you Grandma!" "Thank you friend"; "I'm so glad you are here"; "Feel better"; "You are not alone."

Pictures of loved ones where your children can see them will serve the dual purpose of reminding your children of all those special people who love them and those whom your children can pray for. During a quiet moment you can point to the picture and say, "Let's send a happy thought to Grandpa." The picture will help to focus the thought, reinforce the connection between grandfather and grandchild, and encourage a habit of prayer for others.

THE FEELING OF helplessness we experience when we witness grief and suffering can be banished when we act with love. We can actually change the experience and make it one of expansion, joy, and selflessness for ourselves and our children.

1 J. Donald Walters, adapted from *The Prayer of Saint Francis*
2 Eric Butterworth, contemporary author, Unity minister, considered a leading spokesperson on "practical mysticism"

Chapter 11

We are Spirit

Nurture a spiritual identity.

Our true identity is spirit, not our body or our personality. To have a *spiritual identity* we must accept that connection to spirit and act with that understanding. With a connection to spirit, we can tap into the source of all joy, true happiness, and peace and understand that expanding our awareness into spirit is the way out of pain and fear.

Spiritual identity can also be described as a soul memory of our *potential* in spirit. When children have an understanding of their spiritual identity, they can experience the unchanging spirit within them while everything in the world continually changes. When they have a spiritual identity, they can look at a situation and ask, "What is the *right* thing to do?" rather than "What can *I* do?"

When my two sons were little we would say an affirmation together as part of their bedtime routine: "I am secure in

God's love and light." One evening as I was tucking them in I told them that an adult friend of ours, Paula, was very ill and not expected to live very long. My younger son immediately responded with his understanding that Paula was more than just her physical body and said, "Then we better say the affirmation for her—Paula is secure in God's love and light!"

For our children to live a life of joy, we must nurture that connection with spirit and keep it strong, especially true when scary news and world events threaten to overpower us.

The wonder we sense in young children is that they have a strong sense of their spiritual identity and they express it naturally. As they grow the connection usually becomes weaker because of influence from the outside world, and as adults they can lose sight of it altogether because of personal pain, loss, or fear. For our children to live a life of joy, we must nurture that connection with spirit and keep it strong, especially true when scary news and world events threaten to overpower us. If we wait until difficult times to find a spiritual connection, it may be too little too late.

Finding the Words

When my first son was about three years old, one day he climbed on my lap and said, "Let's talk about God." There I was looking down into his big brown eyes wanting so much to say the right thing that would convey my feelings, let him express his ideas, and leave the door open for future discussions. Many parents find that while they are exploring adulthood, career, and personal interests without children, they are able to put the issue of spirituality on a mental back burner. But when children are in the picture, those issues have a way of coming to the front of the parenting experience. If your children don't ask direct questions about God, they may ask questions about difficult issues like death, poverty, war, sickness, religion, and the uncertain future. Many parents feel unsure about discussing these concepts with adults; to discuss them in terms children will understand is quite a challenge.

The words we use to express our spiritual identity and to teach children about it usually come from the religion we practice, the culture we were raised in, our family traditions, and the experiences we have to draw on. They also carry our biases and expectations. Although the nature of spiritual experience is infinite and varied, the limits of language can make expressing spiritual ideas feel awkward and limited.

Despite the limitations of language, we have to find ways to share our spiritual identity with our children and nurture their spiritual connection each day. Just as we teach children words to describe body parts and emotions, we should provide them with words to describe their spiritual experiences. Words give ideas form and reality.

If you belong to a church or follow a specific teaching, those resources will provide you with a vocabulary to use. Familiar words, stories, and examples help to communicate these important ideas. If you don't have a religion it may be difficult to find the right words. Some parents avoid talking about spiritual ideas because they have turned away from their childhood religions, and discover that the only words they have represent a form they no longer feel connected to.

If you have trouble finding a way to talk with your children about spirituality, try reading together.

If you have trouble finding a way to talk with your children about spirituality, try reading together. Read stories and poems that prompt discussions and help you explore topics you haven't discussed. Talk about the words and ideas used in the stories; eventually you will have a comfortable way of discussing whatever your children are thinking about. For older children, biographies can be particularly inspiring and exciting. And read what your children read, so together you can talk about the characters and their choices and motivations. You will also find plenty of opportunity to discuss how people move toward expansion and light and away from darkness and fear, and the many ways people express their spiritual identity.

My sons are fans of the *Star Wars* movies; those stories have prompted quite a few philosophical and spiritual discussions. The ideas expressed in those stories have become part of our spiritual vocabulary. We find it is easy to talk about fear leading to the "dark side" and our spiritual identity being part of the "force" that connects all creation.

The other side of learning to talk about spirituality is being sensitive about when not to talk about it. True spiritual experiences are deep, personal, and life changing. If you push children to reveal their experiences, they may feel pressured to make up something to please you, or their real experience may feel diminished because of the pressure to share. Let them volunteer their thoughts; respect their privacy when they don't want to.

One evening my son came home from church and I immediately sensed he had something on his mind. He simply looked at me and almost tearfully said, "God spoke to my heart." I hugged him and told him I understood that was all he wanted to say. I was curious, but I knew if he wanted to tell me more, he would.

Experience Means More Than Words

Experiencing expansion of the heart firsthand is the best way to learn which direction to go. We have a practice of praying for others every day during our homeschool. To start us on this new routine, I wrote the names of everyone I could think of to pray for on individual tags and filled a glass jar with names. I got a second glass jar to transfer the names into as we prayed for them. I explained that we would be drawing a name out of the first jar and praying for that person, and then we would place the names in the second jar until we worked through them all. When we went through the jar, we would start again. The children quickly warmed up to the idea and surprised me by eagerly listing more people to pray for, insisting we needed to buy more tags. I had to buy two more packages to take care of their list.

When your children express expansion of the heart and act with a spirit beyond selfish desires, pay close attention.

One morning my daughter pulled out an unfamiliar name. I explained that it was the name of a neighbor boy whom she didn't really know. He was a teenager I had watched grow up from an innocent toddler. Now he appeared to be a troubled young man who walked the streets alone a lot and dressed in black leather and metal chains. He occasionally spoke with my kids, but they were uncomfortable with his appearance and his companions.

My daughter made an unhappy face and asked if she could choose another name. I hesitated just a moment as I considered the options. I didn't want to force her to pray if she was unwilling, but I didn't want to set a precedent that might lead to rejecting other names in the future. I understood her reluctance. She knew this boy as a scary figure dressed in black, who didn't smile or joke with her the way her brothers did. Before I could reply my son offered to trade names with her. I was grateful for his response; it was the perfect example for my daughter and solved my dilemma.

After two months of daily prayer all the names were in the second jar and I dumped them all back in first jar to start again. Almost immediately my daughter again drew the name of the young neighbor. This time she smiled and hung onto the name when I told her who it was. She had experienced an expansion of her sympathies to include a wider circle of people without my lecturing her or forcing her in that direction. It took practice but it happened like the blossoming of a flower, naturally and gracefully.

Suggestions

Reinforce your children's connection with a spiritual identity.

Have you ever looked at your children's behavior, either at home or in public, and cringed at their selfishness and "I-my-me-mine behavior? I certainly have, and I always let my children know how unhappy I am with their behavior. But just as I don't want to define myself by my mistakes, I don't want my children to limit their identities to the mistakes they make.

I once read a story about a toddler trying to stick bandages on his stressed-out mommy, who was crying after work. He couldn't see the owie, but he was trying to fix it. I don't think the author of the article was a parent because there was surprise that a young child was capable of such an act of empathy. Parents see their children's compassion and empathy at a very early age; most parents would not be surprised at the story.

When your children express expansion of the heart and act with a spirit beyond selfish desires, pay close attention. Help them to identify their loving acts as expressions of their spiritual identity so they become more aware of the expansion they feel when that connection is strong. Remember that this expansion is evidence of their true identity. Find opportunities to remind them that selfish, hurtful behavior happens when they forget who they really are.

Create family rituals that reinforce spiritual connections.

The entire family benefits when you come together to share your spiritual connection, although it often takes years for young families to find the rituals and family ceremonies that become woven into the fabric of their life together. Some holiday traditions may be part of your religion, but families also need special celebrations and traditions that are uniquely theirs. These may be the way you bless your meals, the way you celebrate birthdays or mark achievements or welcome the seasons. Don't be afraid to try things and see if they fit your family. If they are a good fit they will become traditions.

During one school year we prayed a gratitude prayer every day to remind ourselves of the source of all our blessings. We said the prayer and then wrote what we were grateful for on a small slip of paper, which we kept in a glass canister so we could see how full it was. Then we took them out and read them on Thanksgiving and again at the end of the year. I still have the canister although we stopped adding to it. We all have fond memories of that ritual and feel a stronger connection with one another because of it. Perhaps we'll do it again someday, or maybe my children will when they are grown and pray with their children. Even now if one child starts the prayer they will all chime in: *We give thanks to God above, for friends and family, life and love. For sun and moon and all the stars, for all we can be, all we are. And for…*

Share your experience more than dogma.

If you are a part of a religious organization, spiritual group, or church, you'll want to share it with your children. The structure and form a group provides gives children different ways to explore spiritual ideas and a language to express spiritual beliefs. From like-minded souls with deeper understanding and broader experience, they will find fellowship and guidance.

Allowing your children to see you express your spiritual identity will have far more impact and meaning than simply learning the dos and don'ts of religious dogma. Include your children in your spiritual life, and they will gain a deeper understanding than is possible with words alone.

A friend once told me that she sometimes would do her evening meditation in her children's room after she tucked them in bed. They loved having her in the room so they would agree to be quiet and still during her meditation. I'm sure it would have been much easier for her to meditate somewhere else, but by including them in her experience they all benefited.

I have another friend who is very enthusiastic and outgoing with her spiritual expression. If she feels inspired, she stops what she is doing and sings a song of praise or even prays out loud. She laughingly shared that she and her kids stopped in the middle of vacuuming one day to sing and pray together. She loves to express her spirituality in art and has taught her children to express their inner spirit in this way, also, with beautiful results.

The headlines and evening news will always show that people are capable of evil, but you will have to show your children that acts of love are even more common and express the reality of our spirit nature.

Our spiritual lives and inner experiences are personal. We usually would not discuss them at the workplace or even with close friends. But our children are looking at us all the time and are learning how to be grown-up people.

If they see us dealing only with the physical world, then that's all they'll learn.

If you feel close to God when you are hiking, tell your children. Share the music you find uplifting or the rituals you draw inspiration from. The point is to reveal your spiritual identity and share the ways you feel connected—not to make them feel the same way. With your example and support, your children will find their own way.

Foster respect for and understanding of the universality of spirit.

I was once in a museum exhibiting a collection of rosary beads; the museum claimed it was the largest collection of its kind in the world. Thousands of beautiful rosaries hung in glass cases, each with a unique history and cataloged by number. As I unexpectedly came around the corner into the display area I immediately felt a change in the atmosphere, as if echoes of all those prayers hung in the air. I was deeply moved. I tried to explain to my children that the rosaries represented hundreds of years of prayer and devotion, but we were distracted by several children loudly pointing out that the beautifully carved figures of saints on the rosaries and in the cases were sinful, according to the religion they practiced at home. I found the parents' silence even more disturbing and sad because they were encouraging an attitude of disrespect, superiority, and exclusiveness in their children.

Respecting other religious practices is a part of teaching that spirituality is universal. Studying world religions may help foster understanding among people, but if intellectual knowledge is not accompanied by a genuine understanding that *spirit* is the reality that connects us all, then there can be no expansion of the heart. It takes an expanded awareness to have compassion and to feel empathy for another's reality. People who deliberately hurt others have contracted their consciousness so much that they feel no connection to a spiritual identity and can't even see the pain they cause.

If you want your children to have a spiritual identity that brings joy into their lives and expands their awareness beyond the small ego, then you must also help them understand that each loving person expresses their connection with spirit in a unique way. When children understand that others have the same need for spiritual connection, they will learn that beneath outer differences they have much in common with them.

Share stories of saints and heroes who have led lives directed by their spiritual identity.

Stories of heroes are always inspiring, even more so when the world seems scary and full of dangers. So many people have experienced terrible fear, have been surrounded by darkness, have faced impossible odds, and still have shown courage, hope, compassion, humor, and kindness. Whether in a lifetime of selfless service or one moment of heroic sacrifice, we have many examples of how one's spiritual identity can direct us toward expansion and joy: Anne Frank, Corrie ten Boom, Joan of Arc, Saint Francis of Assisi, the Dalai Lama, George Washington, Harriet Tubman, Mahatma Gandhi, Moses, and countless others.

The true stories of such people can help show your children what is possible when circumstances seem impossible. They can also illustrate how much we have in common with those who seem to be different and how many ways spirit can be expressed. Make sure your children are exposed to the true stories of heroes and saints; you will all feel inspired, comforted, reassured, and moved.

In a used bookstore I found a large book titled *The American Character* by Norman Vincent Peale. It is composed entirely of short biographies of real people across America who have acted with generosity, compassion, courage, and selflessness. These are ordinary people, not heroes of myth and legend, but their stories are much the same. As my children and I read it together we experienced the conviction that such loving acts of kindness and sacrifice are not extraordinary at all. They are the normal expression of the universal spirit that is our true nature. The headlines and evening news will always show that people are capable of evil, but you will have to show your children that acts of love are even more common and express the reality of our spirit nature.

KEEPING A STRONG SPIRITUAL CONNECTION takes vigilance and persistence. Although spirit itself is deathless and unchanging, it is easily hidden and forgotten under fear, doubt, neglect, and selfish desires. Like a jewel lying on the beach, it will quickly disappear under all the sand of our busy lives. Children help keep our spiritual connection alive, and we have to do the same for them. When my son was about eight years old he confessed, "You seem to think about God a lot—I really don't think about God much at all." I told him that it was okay; it was part of my job to remind him that God never forgot *him*.

Chapter 12

Experiences are Teachers

Gain strength and wisdom from every experience.

Parents want their children to be able to recover after disappointment and hardship. The ability to recover from hardship is usually described as *resilience*, and it is a quality that is valuable in all areas of life. However, when I looked up the definition for *resilient* I found that it also means having the ability to recoil from pressure or shock unchanged or undamaged. Unlike a tree bowing in the wind, resilient people don't often recover from hardship unchanged. I think most parents would expect their children to change with new experiences and hope the changes are for the better. In truth, every experience offers an opportunity to gain strength and wisdom, to change in a positive way, and to move towards love and away from fear.

Change No Circumstance, Change Me

My son's friend Mark has repeatedly disappointed him. After some time apart, Mark called and asked to get together again. I wanted to protect my child from another painful episode so I told him that I didn't think it was a good idea, considering Mark's past behavior. My son said he understood my misgivings, but he had decided he wanted to continue the friendship on *his* terms. He explained that he would spend time with Mark only when Mark sought him out and my son decided it was okay. He knew he couldn't count on Mark, or trust him, but maybe Mark would eventually learn something about friendship from being with him. I was impressed with how he was able to turn his painful experience into an opportunity to give, and was reminded again that growth and learning occur when circumstances challenge us.

One day my younger son noticed the screen saver on my computer, which says, "Change no circumstance Lord, change me." I asked if he understood what it meant and he replied, "I think it means you should try to handle whatever happens and not just wish it didn't happen."

It's natural to want circumstances to change in our favor. We hope the weather will clear before the soccer game, we wish a new job would come along or that we could afford a new car. We pray for peace and we pray for the safety and health of our loved ones. There is nothing wrong about hoping things will improve or taking action to make sure they do. But the fact is that circumstances are *always* changing, and whether they are good or bad is largely a matter of our perspective. If we train our children to look outward at circumstances to keep them happy, they are likely to grow bitter with disappointment and frustration.

I grew up as a U.S. Army brat, moving frequently with my family as my father was transferred to new assignments. Although it was always difficult to leave friends and familiar surroundings, I believed I was lucky to have the experiences I did and saw each move as a new opportunity. But not everyone raised in that lifestyle feels the same. In fact, books have been written about the hardships of military life by those who feel it was the greatest trauma of their childhood and the cause of all the shortcomings in their adult lives. They let themselves become victims of their circumstances rather than growing stronger and wiser through the challenges life offered.

Every experience offers an opportunity to gain strength and wisdom, to change in a positive way, and to move towards love and away from fear.

Every generation looks at the condition of the world and is sure that what it faces is worse than what previous generations had to deal with. In a way it's true—because what challenges us personally will be the most difficult to overcome. But the personal challenges we face are also made to give us what we need to grow stronger emotionally and spiritually. The challenges our children face will offer them opportunities for strength and wisdom, also, but we have to help them recognize the opportunity.

Measuring Our Progress

As we grow and change with our experiences, how do we know if we are making the right changes? How do we measure progress in our children and ourselves? We spend a lot of time teaching children how to measure things like time, distance, money, and the ingredients in chocolate chip cookies. It's natural for children to want to measure themselves, too. They quickly move from comparing physical size to comparing themselves with others; measuring how smart, successful, or worthy they are.

One evening my son came home from a group activity he attends with mixed feelings. He had received a reprimand for his behavior at one point and just a little while later, warm congratulations on passing an exam with 100 percent accuracy. After discussing what had happened, he said he understood why the reprimand was necessary and would not make the same mistake again. He also knew that his study efforts and his father's support had prepared him for the test. Based on outward measures, deciding if the evening had been a success or failure would have been confusing, but a look inward made it very clear. The self-awareness and the understanding of others he gained showed him that the experience was worthwhile and successful in taking him in the right direction.

The most important measure of success is to look within and ask, "Which way am I going?" If your experience is taking you in the direction of more love, toward deeper awareness of God's presence, or an expansion of the heart, you are succeeding. If your experience results in restlessness, anxiety, a contraction of the heart or decrease in compassion and awareness, then you are going in the wrong direction regardless of outward measures of success. Remind your children to look within for confirmation of their success or failure. Support any effort that leads to greater awareness of others and allows love to flow.

Suggestions

In earlier chapters I have referred to ways to help children build emotional and spiritual muscle. Every chapter had suggestions for helping children grow toward joy, love, and wisdom through supportive environment and life experiences. Here some of those suggestions are reviewed or expanded and others added. Refer to chapters for related topics.

Strength in silence (chapters one and three)

The discussions in these chapters relate to understanding all the powerful and negative influences in your children's lives and the importance of creating a home environment that is positive and supportive and that nurtures inner joy. A very important part of that environment should be *silence*. In order to integrate experiences and to learn from them, we need time to reflect, to process our emotions, and to listen to our inner voice of understanding. Without the opportunity to accomplish these tasks, the chances of learning or expanding our awareness are slim.

Children need time for calm reflection as much as adults do. They need silence and quiet activities to nurture their inner life, to learn to be comfortable with themselves, and to awaken their creativity and problem-solving skills. Unfortunately, as most families cope with the demands of their busy lives, quiet time is the first thing neglected. More families are trying to carve out time to be together, but that usually means games, movies, sports, travel, and other worthwhile activities, but no *quiet*. Our media-saturated world intrudes on so much of our family life that we grow accustomed to the voice of the television, radio, electronic games, computer, phone, fax, e-mails, and Internet, yet we forget what the sound of silence is.

Cut back on group activities and outside commitments to make time for your children to relax at home in the quiet. Turn off the electronic voices and let your children learn what their inner voice sounds like. Choose quiet and uplifting music if you find it helpful for inspiring the mood, but even music can interfere when the heart is trying to process emotional experiences and find the path to greater understanding.

Some children may benefit from a daily dedicated quiet time in their schedule. I remember when I was young and out of school during summer vacation, my mother would make my siblings and me take a nap. She would lie down and sleep a little while we protested that we weren't tired. But we were not required to sleep, just to have quiet time. I actually loved the house when it was quiet with the curtains drawn against the bright sunlight. I was "forced" to lie in bed and ponder whatever thoughts came my way. It was such a lovely break from all the demands of childhood.

My children all love quiet time in varying doses (which rarely coincides with *my* need for quiet!). Coordinating the individual needs of several children can be tricky, but the important thing is to make it a priority and help your children by not interfering when quiet reigns. Fight the urge to get them to do something if they don't appear to be doing anything productive. If the TV and electronic devices are off and they are drawing, building, creating, or just thinking, leave them alone to do it. They will learn where the solutions to problems come from, where ideas become clear, and where the heart can open to let love flow through—in silence.

Cultivate self-confidence (chapter two)

Children are more likely to develop confidence in their abilities if they are not overwhelmed with scary information that is beyond their understanding and ability to deal with. Use the criteria in chapter 2 to decide what your children need to be exposed to. Help them develop emotional and mental muscles in reasonable steps that are appropriate for their ages and development.

In *The Wonderful Wizard of Oz* by L. Frank Baum, Dorothy has the power—with her magical ruby slippers, to go home, but she doesn't know it. The wicked witch is able to hold her captive simply because Dorothy is also ignorant of the protection offered by Glenda, the good witch. Dorothy's fearful adventures would have been a lot shorter had she only understood the power she had!

Tell your children that they have the inner strength to cope with all kinds of challenges. When they are uncertain or afraid, listen and acknowledge their feelings, but remind them of their past achievements as well as the strength they gained from all experiences, even if those experiences were seen as failures.

A friend, the director of a private school, related a story about one of her teachers and a student who couldn't contain her excitement about opening the window on the class advent calendar. The student interrupted the teacher several times and disrupted the lesson. She knew she was out of control and said, "I just can't help it!" But her teacher reassured her gently that she was a powerful little girl and she *did* have the power to control her talking. Then she excused the student from the room and gave her the opportunity to take a moment alone to calm herself. Within a few minutes the student quietly came back and took her seat. What a wonderful gift that teacher gave her student—the confidence in her own inner power.

Friends help us learn and grow (chapter four)

Friends are the greatest asset anyone can have to help them cope with scary news and daily challenges. Without my husband and my other friends I wouldn't have the strength to deal with everything I must do each day. Also, it would be very difficult to gain wisdom from my experiences without being able to share them with friends.

Childhood friendships are different from adult friendships, but children use friends to learn about the world and about themselves, too. Friends give children a forum for expression and a way to test ideas safely.

Parents are the greatest influence in children's lives.

Listening to a friend's reaction to ideas and hearing theirs is one of the most valuable ways we learn.

One afternoon, I overheard a conversation between two friends who were on the porch coloring with my children. One girl asked a younger boy what he was going to be when he grew up. He told her that he didn't know yet, but God would tell him what he should do when he was older. The older girl immediately responded that it didn't work that way, that God doesn't tell people what they are supposed to be. Instead of being intimidated by the older girl, who seemed to know what she was talking about, the young boy firmly said, "Yes–He does!" She argued, "No–He doesn't!" The arguing continued for several moments and I listened to hear the outcome. Suddenly the girl gave a little sigh and said respectfully, "Okay, if that's what you think, that's okay." The boy nodded his head in acknowledgment and continued coloring.

That conversation offered both children an opportunity to express their opinions and stand firm, despite opposition.

It was a chance to learn self-confidence and respect for others. By voicing their opinions, they discovered how they felt on an issue and learned more about themselves. They will handle future challenges using the inner strength and understanding they gained that day.

Every friendship your children develop offers enormous possibilities for growth and expanded awareness. Help them nurture their friendships and reap the rewards true friendships bring.

You have power as a parent (chapter five)

Parents are the greatest influence in children's lives. Your support can help them look at a situation without fear and choose a response. In addition, if you are able to respond to stressful events as an opportunity for growth and deeper understanding, your example will naturally lead them in the right direction.

Children can learn a great deal from our mistakes, too, if we are willing to acknowledge and share them. I remember being angry one afternoon when I got in the car with my young son, and because I was preoccupied and emotional I took the wrong route and drove a considerable distance out of my way. When I realized my mistake I told my son, "See, this is the kind of thing that happens when I indulge in anger. My brain doesn't even function and I can't think clearly at all." On another occasion, months later, I found myself on the road with my son and again I was upset about something. This time my son piped up from the back seat, "Remember what happens to your brain when you're angry, Mom!"

Sharing your history with your children and how you learned from adversity can be valuable, too, if it is done with humility and not with a desire to prove that their challenges are small by comparison.

When I was a teenager my mother told me stories and explained things I had never heard her speak of in my presence. She must have felt I was old enough to understand. Her experiences as a young woman during World War II made such an impression on me that I never looked at my life in the same way again. I still draw on her example to help me cope when my life feels difficult.

Trust the inner voice (chapters six and seven)

Chapter 6 is about identifying real threats and choosing how to respond with love as a guide. Chapter seven includes discussions about assessing risks and balancing intellectual understanding with inner guidance. Learning to trust our inner voice and letting it lead us to greater awareness, wisdom, and strength is a lifelong process requiring a great deal of practice. As with most important lessons, *experience* is the most effective teacher.

Remember the cartoons with the little devil on one shoulder and a little angel on the other, each whispering in an ear? The options were always presented as clear and simple: good or bad. In my life the options don't always seem so clear, and there usually seem to be many more than just two. The choices children need to make may not appear as weighty as ours, so we sometimes lose patience when they agonize over seemingly trivial decisions. But we can help give them a great source of strength and wisdom if we understand that every choice made creates an experience they can draw on when faced with more important choices.

To grow stronger and wiser from our mistakes, we need to forgive ourselves and accept responsibility without becoming that mistake.

Between the ages of about four and eight, my son had great difficulty making decisions. When choosing a new toy or an activity or a snack, he focused so much on what he would lose by choosing that he was miserable. I often lost patience because the problem affected all of us, and sometimes I tried to control things to prevent him from having to make a decision. But I also knew that practice is essential to improve any skill, so the family would try to support him as he suffered through every choice.

Progress was gradual, but he eventually learned to be more comfortable with making choices and living with the consequences. Although he would ask the advice of others, he learned to listen to his inner guidance and trust it. He also had to understand that mourning over the roads not taken robbed him of joy in the present. One day after spending his money on a toy he said, "Remember when I couldn't even decide what to do? I'm much better at that now. I'm really happy with my decision!" His experience has also given him empathy for both children and adults who have trouble making decisions. He will sympathize and offer advice because he understands. There was a time I was afraid he would have a lifelong problem that would cause him much grief; now I see a strength and understanding that will serve him well when the stakes are much higher.

Willingly give yourself to every challenge (chapter eight)

During one lesson with my children about Michelangelo I didn't think they understood how challenging it must have been to paint the Sistine Chapel ceiling. So I had them lie on the floor while I held a large cookie sheet about twelve inches above their heads. Then I told them to pretend to paint on the cookie sheet, as if it were the ceiling. After just a short time they complained that their arms hurt and the floor was hard. We then talked about how difficult it must have been to lie on a scaffold for hours and paint a beautiful picture. We concluded that the most important part of concentration is willingness. If you really *want* to do something, it is easier to concentrate and overcome obstacles.

When we willingly give all we can to each challenge we can gain enormous strength and wisdom from the experience. If we waste our energy worrying about the future or regretting the past, we will never know our true potential for success. Like an army facing battle, if half the forces run away, the chances of winning are slim. When we feel joy and enthusiasm for an activity, it is because all of our mental soldiers are working together and we can feel the power of all that energy moving in one direction.

Have a sense of humor (chapter nine)

Noticing beauty and goodness in the world should also help us to laugh and see the humor in our lives. I love this quote from W.E.B. DuBois[1] that expresses it so clearly:

> *I am especially glad of the divine gift of laughter; it has made the world human and loveable, despite all its pain and wrong.*

Humor helps us to gain perspective on our difficulties and enables us to experience more joy. Sharing humor helps us recognize and deepen our connection to others.

Children can be very sensitive to being laughed *at*, just as adults are. Teach your children to use humor with kindness and sensitivity to the feelings of others. Helping them to see the humor in life and using humor to comfort and heal are wonderful ways to build emotional and spiritual muscle.

Serve others (chapter ten)

Serving others is one of the most effective ways to help children gain strength and wisdom while they learn more about themselves and connect with others. Helping others makes children and adults feel *bigger* inside; it gives us a sense of accomplishment and contribution, and we feel our fears shrink as love grows. Take any opportunity to help your children experience that true service means acting with love for others.

On more than one occasion my children have come to me and asked, "Can I go over to my friend's house and help clean his room?" I'll laugh and suggest they come back home afterward and work on their own room. They will always give me an exasperated look and say, "That's different, Mom." It *is* different when we are helping someone else. Part of the reason is that the presence of a friend helps work seem fun, but the deeper truth is that it is natural for our hearts to open and more love to flow through us when we serve others willingly. We naturally respond to that flow of divine love, and we gain strength from the blessings.

We can also gain a deeper understanding of the power of service when we are the recipients of the loving actions of others. My family was surprised while eating at a restaurant one evening when the waitress came to our table and told us another patron had purchased a pie for us. The woman had paid for the pie and instructed the waitress to let us choose which kind we wanted, then left the restaurant before we were able to know who she was. We were all touched by the generosity of the stranger and we had a fun and valuable discussion about why she had given the gift anonymously, to people she didn't know.

We can counteract the contraction of the heart that happens with fear and anxiety by reaching out to others and serving in any way we can. We can show our children how to open their hearts and experience more love and joy through service.

Forgive yourself (chapter eleven)

Guilt and regret are heavy burdens that can prevent us from gaining anything from trials and hardship. In chapter eleven spiritual identity was described as a soul memory of our *potential* in spirit. In other words, when we identify the self as spirit, we understand that our ignorance and our mistakes do not define who we are. Our children need to learn that guilt and regret over mistakes will not help them learn or grow any wiser. When they make mistakes they may need to make amends, to face the consequences, or to ask for forgiveness, but then they must change their behavior and move on.

To grow stronger and wiser from our mistakes, we need to forgive ourselves and accept responsibility without *becoming* that mistake. If you remind your children that they truly are spiritual beings, then they will come to understand that their mistakes are like curtains over a beautiful stained glass window: if you just look underneath you will see the light shining through. The same is true for adults of course. We won't handle every situation as well as we could; we will make mistakes. Our mistakes should offer us opportunities to learn and grow. Sometimes I need to make the same mistake *many* times before I learn, but every time is another opportunity.

THE LIFE EXPERIENCES our children will encounter will change them. We hope every experience gives them greater strength and wisdom and they learn that a joyful life is of their own making and not dependent on outward circumstances. Resilience comes when we learn to measure our success by looking within and we accept challenges willingly.

1 William Edward Burghardt DuBois, 1868-1963 American educator, editor, writer and activist, founder of the NAACP

Conclusion

As today's scary news fades, new dreadful headlines will appear. The issue of raising children with joy and overcoming fear will not go away in the foreseeable future. I believe our children will see many changes *for the better* in their lifetimes: Wonderful technological advances, greater cultural understanding, and conveniences that will add enjoyment to family life. But the speed of dark will also advance and affect lives in ways we cannot foresee. The scary news and frightening headlines offer a challenge for all of us: to grow in truth and light and to experience inner joy no matter the outward circumstances. For parents, the headlines and negative messages are a continual reminder of the dangers waiting for our children. But we are not helpless; we can teach them to be guided by love instead of by fear. We can protect them from harsh realities while they grow and gradually prepare them to live in an uncertain and dangerous world. We can give them experiences of beauty, peace, and joyful appreciation, which will give them inner strength to draw on when needed.

As the most powerful influence in the lives of children, parents have a great burden of responsibility—and a wonderful opportunity.

Our children will look to us for reassurance, for information and for comfort. We can do so much by being with them and providing a home that is a peaceful haven when the world becomes confusing and frightening. The love and support of good friends will provide nourishment and strength for the positive outlook we encourage at home and try to maintain in our busy, complex lives. We can show by our example that taking action with love for others is the best way to fight fear and helplessness.

The opportunities we provide our children will help them learn to make decisions and defend themselves when necessary. They will learn to depend not on intellectual assessment alone, but to trust their inner guidance and follow where love leads them. With each experience they will gain wisdom and inner strength to help them face whatever challenges they must in the years ahead.

The greatest gift we can give our children is the assurance that their true identity is unchanging spirit, created in divine joy, and on this truth they can stand unshaken in an unpredictable and chaotic world.

AS THE MOST POWERFUL influence in the lives of children, parents have a great burden of responsibility—and a wonderful opportunity. We need to show our children how they can experience the joy of life while being very aware of its dangers. The truly wonderful part is that we can experience life's joys *with* our children and grow with them while together our family invites more light, love, and hope into our lives.

A Quick List
12 things you can do today

1. Look at the environment from a child's view; be aware of all sources of negative, confusing or frightening information.

2. Turn off the radio in your car when children are present.

3. Control all sources of information and possible scary news in your own home.

4. Keep company with people who are good examples for your children.

5. Be with your children as much as possible.

6. Pray with your children.

7. Answer your children's questions about scary news honestly, giving facts, reassurance of safety, and ideas for positive action.

8. Notice beauty and goodness and experience the joy of today with your children.

9. Do something with love for another person.

10. Give your children quiet time.

11. Remind yourself and your children that we all are spiritual beings.

12. Listen to your inner guidance.

Related Resources

A Terrible Thing Happened
A Story for Children Who Have Witnessed Violence or Trauma
Margaret Holmes, illustrated by Cary Pillo
Magination Press/American Psychological Association, 2000
A picture book to read with children, reading level is for 4—8 year olds. This presents a gentle way to acknowledge children's feelings and encourage them to talk about what scares them. The content is not specific and can be used to discuss many kinds of fears.

Bad Stuff in the News
A Guide to Handling the Headlines
Rabbi Marc Gellman and Monsignor Thomas Hartman
SeaStar Books, 2002
Written for teens, grades 6—10, this book addresses many difficult issues that children may have questions about and gives suggestions for positive things children can do to comfort themselves and help others.

Brighter Baby
Jay Gordon, M.D. and Brenda Adderly, M.H.A.
Lifeline Press, 1999
Written for parents who want to positively influence their children's early development and maximize their learning potential. Emphasizes active, loving parental involvement and techniques like infant massage to enhance bonding.

Dr Dave's Cyberhood
Making Media Choices that Create a Healthy Electronic Environment for Your Kids
David Walsh, Ph.D.
Simon and Schuster, 2001
Practical advice for parents to stay informed and involved when choosing the electronic environments where kids play and learn.

Jenny is Scared!
When Sad Things Happen in the World
Carol Shuman, illustrated by Cary Pillo
Magination Press/American Psychological Association, 2003
A picture book to read with children, reading level is for four–eight year olds. Explores children's fears, and reactions surrounding terrorism, war, and other violent events in the world.

Raising Resilient Children:
Fostering Strength, Hope, and Optimism in Your Child and *Nurturing Resilience in Our Children: Answers to the Most Important Parenting Questions*
Robert Brooks, Ph.D. and Sam Goldstein, Ph.D.
Contemporary Books, 2001
An in-depth examination of why some children are able to overcome enormous challenges and others become victims of early experiences. The second book responds in more detail to parent's questions on this topic.

Saving Childhood:
Protecting Our Children from the National Assault on Innocence
Michael Medved and Diane Medved, Ph.D.
HarperCollins, 1998
Explains how the media, schools, peers, and parents contribute to children's loss of innocence and how parents can defend their children by giving them security and encouraging their sense of wonder and optimism.

The Worried Child
Recognizing Anxiety in Children and Helping Them Heal
Paul Foxman, Ph.D.
Hunter House Publishers, 2004
This book provides detailed information for parents regarding the causes and the effects of anxiety in children, anxiety disorders and treatment, and includes many suggestions for how parents can help.

Internet Sites

www.kidsnewsroom.org This site was designed by parents and offers a wonderful, kid-friendly way to learn about current events. Children can write and submit their own articles about featured stories, play games, and look up topics of interest.

> *Always check out internet sites before allowing children access.

www.grief.net A site with an incredible array of resources regarding grief and recovery. There is information to help you through your own grief, resources for learning how to help others, and tools for helping children who are experiencing a loss.

www.maginationpress.com This site contains information about books published for children by the American Psychological Association. Titles include *Jenny is Scared* and *When Terrible Things Happen* and others addressing special concerns that affect children.

www.fema.gov/kids The Federal Emergency Management Agency's site for kids. Contains accurate and useful information about disaster preparedness, disaster relief, and recovery in a kid-friendly format. This is a great site for the whole family to explore and learn from together. *Always check out internet sites before allowing children access.

Acknowledgements

Every parent and every child I have had the privilege to know has contributed to this book in some way and I thank them all for the experiences they have given me. I have been blessed with dear friends, Susan Dermond and Debra Kate, who helped make sure this book became a practical tool for helping others. Many thanks to Beth Shiffman, Angela MacMahon, Lisa DelBondio, Pam and John Vredevelt, and my entire homeschool mother's support group. The deepest love and gratitude to my parents, Carl, Daniel, Timothy, Mary, and my extended spiritual family who have taught me that there is always more love to be shared.

Notes ———————

Notes ───────────

Notes ——————————

Notes ─────────────

Notes ———————————

About the Author

Lorna Knox is an extraordinary teacher and has found ways to use her talents as a teacher outside of the conventional classroom.

As a nurse and health educator for 15 years, she taught people about health issues, pregnancy and child care. As a homeschool parent and an active member of her church, she created curriculum and explored practical and fun ways to teach spiritual concepts to children of all ages.

Lorna lived around the U.S., in Europe, and Asia while growing up, which allowed her to experience world cultures and spiritual teachings. She now calls the Pacific Northwest home and lives in Portland, Oregon with her husband and three children. When she is not writing, Lorna is busy homeschooling and teaching classes on spiritual parenting topics.

Visit Lorna's web site at www.joyfulchildren.com
Contact Lorna at lornaknox@joyfulchildren.com

advice, letting children offer you, 94
affection. See touch
Alexander, Cecil, 117
amends, making, 108
angels, 58–59
animals, 136
appreciation, 120–21
attitudes, negative, 41, 42

basic needs, 18
beauty, 111, 116–18, 122; is everywhere, 112–13, 125; listening children's moments of, 119–20; making room for, 113–15, 120–21; in one's home, 38; opportunities for children to experience, 119
bedtime, 59–60. See also prayer
bliss, 124. See also joy
body language, 20
brain: connections among areas of, 18, 76; experience and the, 17–19; plasticity, 18–19, 21; shaping neural pathways, 21–23
Brazelton, Terry, 19
Brooks, Robert, 52
Burnett, Frances Hodgson, 118
Butterworth, Eric, 127

calendar, 109
"cartoon physics", 96
change, met with optimism, 74, 76
changing oneself, 156–58
children: behavior of, as barometer, 47; concerns about negative influences on, ix; having their own area/space, 35–37; protecting their minds, 14–27; shielding them from harsher realities of life, 14
choosing the right action, 131–33. See also decisions; discriminating
Coleridge, Samuel Taylor, 139
collections of beauty and goodness, 120

comfort: looking to other adults for, 80; need for, 50–65; from unseen helpers, 58–59
communication technology, history of, 4–7
computer usage, 11
concentration, 103–6
consciousness, training one's, 116–18
control, 74
conversations with spouse and friends, 34
courage, 74

Darwin, Charles, 69–71
decisions, 97; based on love vs. fear, xi, 75–76; explaining the reason for, 93–94; including children in, 80; letting children make and experience consequences of, 95; letting children see you struggle with, 94. See also choosing the right action; discriminating; inner guidance; risk(s)
decorating one's home, 36
depression, 9–10
developmental cues, 16–17
developmental stages, 26–27
discriminating skills and choices, 72–74
discrimination, 81–84
DuBois, William Edward Burghardt, 168

educating children. See information
electronic mail (e-mail), 5
emotional baggage vs. mental muscle, information as, 23–24
emotions: and the brain, 19; and information, 7–10; as organizers, 19–20. See also feelings
empathy, 61
environment: creating a joyful and

optimistic, 35–40, 123–24; minimizing ugliness in, 120–21; paying attention to, 39. See also home events: coping with unanticipated, 109; planning for, 109. See also surprises
experience: means more than words, 145–47; as opportunity and teacher, 155, 157

facial expressions, 20
failures, 170
fear, x–xi, 109–10; decisions based on love vs., xi, 75–76. See also scary news
feelings: children listening to their, 39, 48 (see also inner guidance); honesty about one's, 53, 78; listening to children's, 53, 61. See also emotions
fight or flight mechanism, 69–72
forgiving oneself, 170
Foxman, Paul, 74
friends, 41–42; children hearing conversations between adult, 34; children's, 34; choosing, 42–43, 47, 49; encouraging loving gestures toward, 48–49; imaginary, 58–59; influence of, 41–46, 162–64; as protection, 46; and scary news, 46; some will not be forever, 49; talking in front of children, 32–33; variety of, 49
friendship, including children in one's acts of, 47–48
fun days, 109. See also joy
fundraising, 136–37
future, worry about the: helping children put aside, 109–10. See also presence

giving. See love
God, 107, 142, 154; love of,

127–28; talking about, 143
Goldstein, Sam, 52
goodness, 120, 122; making room for, 113–15; reminding children of, 124–25
Gordon, Jay, 22
gratitude, 120–21
gratitude prayer, example of, 149
greed, 123–24. See also money
grief, 108–9, 128–29, 140
Grief Recovery Institute, 61
guilt, 132, 170
Gunnar, Megan, 8, 68

heart. See spiritual identity
heroes, sharing stories of, 152–53
home: decluttering and beautifying one's, 38; decorating one's, 36; "home sweet home," 30–31; as (safe) haven, 28–39; safety precautions in, 62. See also environment
honesty about one's feelings, 53, 78
humor, sense of, 168

imaginary friends, 58–59
information: as emotional baggage vs. mental muscle, 23–24; emotions and, 7–10, 25–26; in home (see home); not overloading children with too much, 79–80; as opportunity for growth, 25–26; sharing (with children), 25–27, 79–80; teaching about reliable sources of, 80
inner guidance, 48, 86–88, 96–97, 165–67. See also feelings
Internet, 5
intuition. See inner guidance

joy, 22, 89, 113, 124; choosing to live joyfully, 70, 72; listening to children share moments of, 119–20;

moving toward, 89–91; skills to
balance scary realities with, 9, 10.
See also beauty

letters, sending, 135–36
Lewis, C. S., 98–99
listening: to children share moments
of joy and beauty, 119–20; to children's feelings, 53, 61; to the heart
(*see* inner guidance)
loss, 108–9, 135–36. *See also* grief
love, 126; acting with, 131–33,
135–38, 168–69; decisions based on
fear vs., xi, 75–76; giving a memory
of, 128–30; infinite source of,
127–28; nature of, 126, 127. *See
also* spiritual identity
love objects, need for, 57–58

magazine covers, 11
magazines, 32
Maslow, Abraham, 18
Medved, Diane, 15
Medved, Michael, 15
mementos, 35
memories, organizing, 20, 128
mental muscle vs. emotional baggage, information as, 23–24
mistakes, 170
money, 133–35, 137; as energy in
disguise, 133, 134. *See also* greed

nature: bringing it indoors, 38
needs, hierarchy of, 18
negative attitudes, 41, 42
news: listening to the, 31–32; talking about how it is presented,
81–83
newspaper pictures, 11, 32
newspapers, 32
9/11, 20, 124, 129–30

parental presence, power of, 51–54,
164–65
past, worry about the: helping children put aside, 107–9. *See also*
presence
Peale, Norman Vincent, 153
pictures, 135–36; of family and
friends, 35, 139–40
positive action, giving ideas for, 79
power, cultivating one's, 161–62
prayer, 56, 63–65, 107, 138–40,
148–49
presence, parental, 51–54, 164–65
present: being in the moment,
101–3; living in the, 98–99, 110;
teaching children to savor the, 110.
See also future; past
progress, measuring, 158–59

quiet activities, 60
quite time, 159–61

radio, 4–5; listening to, 31–32. *See
also* news
reassurance, 79
relaxation, 159–61
religion. *See* God; spirit/spirituality
resilience, 52, 74, 155
responsibility: taking (see changing
oneself)
risk(s): assessing, 88–90, 95–96;
taking, 90–93
risky activities portrayed on TV, 96
rooms, child's, 35–36; making it a
special, personal place, 36–37; television in, 37–38
routine, power of, 54–55

safety. *See* under home
saints, sharing stories of, 152–53
scary news, x–xii, 4, 172; impact on
children, 16–17; limiting exposure

to, 23–25, 31–35; paucity of facts and diversity of responses regarding, 81; resolving, 62–63; sharing positive stories that relate to, 34; timing of, 59–60; various responses to, 81; what to tell children regarding, xii; when you have to respond to, 77–78
scheduling, 54–55
school: messages children are exposed to in, 12; parental involvement with, 33
school materials, previewing, 33
self-confidence, cultivating, 161–62
September 11, 2001, 20, 124, 129–30
serving others. *See* love, acting with
silence, strength in, 159–61
speed of dark, 3–7
spirit/spirituality, 58–59, 122, 145–47, 154; attitude of the, 99–101; fostering respect for universality of, 151–52; sharing experience rather than dogma, 149–51. *See also* inner guidance
spiritual connections, family rituals that reinforce, 148–49
spiritual identity, 152, 173; nurturing, 141–42, 147–48; sharing stories of lives led by, 152–53; talking about, 143–45
stories, sharing, 34, 152–53
stress, 8, 68–69; defined, 8, 68
stress response, 21, 52, 76. *See also* fight or flight mechanism
surprises, 109–10. *See also* events

talking, provides comfort, 59–60
television, 5, 11, 96. *See also* news
television programs, previewing, 33
Tennyson, Alfred, 138
Teresa, Mother, 122, 125, 133
touch, power of, 55–57
traditions, family, 148–49

video games, 96
vulnerability, emotional, 16–17

Walsh, David, 10–11
Wilder, Laura Ingalls, 104–5
Wizard of Oz, The (Baum), 161–62
world as unsafe, 28–30

I Came From Joy!

Spiritual Affirmations and Activities for Children
By Lorna Knox

This beautifully conceived, non-sectarian tool for developing a child's inner, spiritual life—ideal for parents, teachers, youth group leaders, and religious educators. Written for children age 5-11, but adaptable for all ages, *I Came From Joy!* offers fun and uplifting exercises that teach children 26 values including kindness, love, concentration, happiness, discrimination, sharing, patience, security, and how to be a success. This workbook includes full lesson plans, reproducible picture pages, guidance on how to teach spiritual values, and a list of recommended books and resources.

I Came From Joy! music CD

Music to Make Your Heart Sing!
Sung by the Joy Singers
CD: 7-98499-50232-6

Featuring songs referenced in the book *I Came From Joy!*, this delightful recording can be used in conjunction with the book, or listened to by itself. This music will encourage happiness and self-worth in children throughout the pre-school and primary years.

For Goodness Sake

Supporting Children and Teens in Discovering Life's Higher values
By Michael Nitai Deranja

Today, many parents and teachers are at a loss when it comes to encouraging values in children. Old-style methods of indoctrination and authoritarian pressure seem increasingly out-of-place in a world calling for greater openness to new ideas and diverse cultures. Yet the need for positive values remains, in some ways more urgently than ever given the often-harmful influences of the modern media. In the midst of this moral vacuum, Deranja, a parent and schoolteacher for over 30 years, offers a refreshingly new perspective on this age-old challenge. Through a wide variety of games, stories, and other hands-on activities, he shows how to engage young people in the exploration of such values as kindness, cheerfulness, courage, willingness, and self-control. Then, based upon their own experience, children and teens can discover the practical benefits of these important qualities and appreciate the wisdom of incorporating them in their daily lives.

Education for Life

Preparing Children to Meet the Challenges
By J. Donald Walters

Here is a constructive alternative to modern education. The author stresses spiritual values and helping children grow toward full maturity learning not only facts, but also innovative principles for better living. This book is the basis for the Living Wisdom schools and the Education for Life Foundation, which trains teachers, parents and educators. Encouraging parents and educators to see children through their soul qualities, this unique system promises to be a much needed breath of fresh air.

Little Secrets Gift Books

Little Secrets of Happiness
Little Secrets of Friendship
Life's Little Secrets
Little Secrets of Success

Each Secrets book is a collection of profound thoughts, one for each day of the month. Here you'll find wise guidance for living with courage and grace, as well as warm comfort for life's inevitable ups and downs geared towards children. Simply and beautifully designed to be a gift of lasting value, these inspirational guides to living have become best-selling gifts, with nearly one million copies in print.